CLEAR YOUR HEAD TRASH

How to Create Clarity, Peace & Confidence in Your
Life & Work

ALEXIA LEACHMAN

mankai media

Published by Mankai Media, UK.

For permission requests or bulk orders contact the publisher by writing to hello@mankaimedia.com

Visit the author's websites at www.clearmyheadtrash.com and www.alexialeachman.com

First edition.

ISBN 978-1-9998915-3-4

Disclaimer: The Head Trash Clearance method is a self-help method that quite often produces incredible results with amazing benefits, which may be both physical and emotional in nature. However, it is a relatively new self-help method and has not been thoroughly studied.

This book is based on the personal observations and experiences of Alexia Leachman. You, the reader, must take 100% responsibility for your own health, both physical and emotional. The Head Trash Clearance Method should not be misconstrued or used to diagnose the presence or absence of any particular mental, physical or emotional ailment.

This book is not intended to be a substitute for the services of any health care professional. Neither the author nor the publisher is responsible for any consequences incurred by those employing the remedies or treatments discussed or taught herein. Any application of the material shared within this book is at the reader's discretion and is his or her sole responsibility.

The stories in this book are all true, but the names have been changed in some circumstances to protect privacy.

Every effort has been made to ensure all information in this book is correct. Any unintended error will be corrected in the next edition.

Credits: Book cover design by Lex Knox and editing by Wayne H. Purdin

For everyone who's pushed my buttons.
Thank you!

If you have good thoughts, they will shine out of your face like sunbeams and you will always look lovely.

Roald Dahl

Contents

Introduction

In today's world, life is a total stress-fest. We're bombarded with things vying for our attention. "Labour saving" devices that we scramble to buy are actually making us even more busy, and we rarely get the opportunity to switch off. Our addiction to screens means that we don't even get any quiet time anymore, time to just sit and gaze at nature or close our eyes. We have no time to process how we're feeling. Urbanisation means we get less exposure to nature, something that we know can help us to relax and decompress. More and more people are suffering from stress, anxiety, and depression. Suicide rates are escalating, and social media just makes it worse. Even the kids can't escape all this. In a nutshell: we're buggered!

Our head space is under fire and we have nowhere to retreat to, and it's costing us dearly. We're more physically ill than we've ever been. We work harder than we ever did, and mental health issues are on the rise. This has got to stop! But how do we stop this? How does one person, YOU, stop this, at least in your own life? Because that's all we can do, right? The only thing we can do is make changes to ourselves; changing seven billion other people is way too much for anyone's to-do list right now. Even changing one other person is too much. If I said to you that this is sortable, would you believe me? Well, if you give me a chance, I'd like to show you how.

If you're feeling overrun with challenging emotions that just seem to get in the way of you enjoying life, then this is probably not the first book you've read on the subject. I'm going out on a limb here, but I reckon that once or twice, you've probably come across something saying that "change starts within," "change yourself to change others," "be the change you want to see in the world," blah blah blah.... We've all read this stuff. Well, I hate to break it to you, but it's true. But what's less obvious when this well-sounding advice is dished out is HOW to do this EXACTLY. When I've read this stuff, I'm one of those people nodding enthusiastically at the idea that I need to change myself. I'm up for it; I really am. JUST SHOW ME WHAT I NEED TO DO! Step-by-frigging-step! Please.

Well, my friend, your search is up! In this book, I'm going to show you how you can calm the chatter in your head and create some head space. EXACTLY. Step-by-step. You're going to learn how to clear your head trash: all that stuff in your head that's stressing you out and keeping you up at night. This book is for people who are up for changing themselves and just want to know what to do. This book is for you if you struggle with voices in your head: the anxieties, the stresses, the conflicts, and the endless mental replays. This book is definitely for you if you've decided that the time is up on that crap; enough is enough. Let's sort this!

As someone who's been clearing her head trash for what seems like forever, I've picked up a few shortcuts. About ten years ago, I was a total mess. Life threw me a huge curveball and it got the better of me. The need to sort my head out immediately moved from the "Do Someday" pile to my "URGENT - Do It NOW!" pile. It was do or die for me, quite literally. Over the years, I had tried all sorts of techniques and approaches in my attempt to get my head space to a calmer place where I had clarity, confidence, motivation, and direction, but these things still eluded me. Until I discovered what I'm going to share with you in this book.

I first stumbled across what I'm going to share with you when I was a business coach. I had decided to train in some mindset techniques because I was quickly seeing that mindset was the biggie that determined whether my clients succeeded in achieving the goals they'd come to me for support with. And, to be honest, I needed to learn some mindset tricks for myself! I'm a firm believer in walking the talk, so if I was to help others with their mindset, I sure as hell needed to have done some work on my own. Around this time, my life went down a sinkhole - for reasons I'll elaborate on later - so I had a double dose of head trash to deal with; the regular stuff I pick up through daily life, and my crappy life curveball.

Then one day, with this as a delightful backdrop, one of my Big Life Tests showed up; I found out I was pregnant. What made this a big deal was that becoming pregnant highlighted to me that I had tokophobia, the extreme fear of birth and pregnancy. I didn't even know such a thing existed until I experienced the sickening fear and utter dread I felt on seeing that blue line. This took on a whole new dimension when I found out that I miscarried and had lost the baby; I was relieved. Gutted, but relieved. I don't know about you, but this isn't a healthy maternal response, at least not in my world. For me, this was a sign that I had head trash on a monumental scale and I needed to sort it out.

I spent the subsequent year clearing out my head trash like a woman possessed. By the time I became pregnant again a year later, I had managed to move on from my anxiety-ridden existence. But I still had The Fear, and now I had an immovable deadline hurtling towards me. This was not the time to put my head trash clearance on hold; quite the opposite.

During my second trimester, I managed to clear all my pregnancy and birth fears to the point that my original plan of having a C-section - to avoid the pain of childbirth - was ditched in favour of a home birth. I had my first daughter at home and incredibly, it was pain-free. Fluke, right? At least that's what my head trash was telling me. So four years later when I was pregnant again, I was tested. Was it fluke? Did my head trash clearance really work? Could I do it again? Happily, the birth went brilliantly again. In fact it was even better, which wasn't what I was expecting! Word got out about my fearful to fearless transformation, and, in the first few weeks of my second daughter's life, I started getting emails from women I didn't even know, asking me how I did it. The emails got to the point where I thought it would be quicker to write a book, which I did. That book is *Fearless Birthing: Clear Your Fears for a Positive Birth*. In waiting for the book to get from draft to published state I launched my *Fear Free Childbirth* podcast so that I could share how I did it and, at the very least, help the women who had emailed me!

I thought that that would be it and that now I could get back to being a business coach and write THIS book. I had been talking about writing this book for years, and I had decided that I would do it during my maternity leave, but I got sidetracked. The *Fear Free Childbirth* podcast took on a life of its own, and I started getting emails from women all over the world, telling me how what I was sharing with them - what I'm going be to sharing with you in this book - was changing their whole mindset. Women who were fearful like I was were going on to have incredible positive birth experiences after clearing their head trash. Today, the *Fear Free Childbirth* podcast has been downloaded more than 400,000 times in over 180 countries and I've supported thousands of women in shifting their mindset and letting go of their fears, anxieties, and traumas around birth. The thing is, the clearance method that I'm going to teach you isn't limited to birth stuff; it can be used on ANY type of head trash, and that's why I've finally got back to getting this damn book finished.

People everywhere are stressed like crazy and, more than anything, they want to find some kind of peace. They want to calm the chatter in their minds and create some head space. When you lighten the load in your head and have the space to think, magic happens. You're able to think clearly and tune into what matters. Your intuition comes alive and guides you towards those things that will bring you fulfilment in your life. You're able to just BE, without the need for incessant distractions. You're able to make life choices from the heart and not from a place of fear. Your health picks up as your body stops taking the hit for your emotional disease. Happiness is something that's in the now and not some future goal. This is what's waiting for you once you create some head space... Isn't that something worth focusing on to achieve?

And do you want to know the great news? This doesn't have to take forever. This is something that's within easy grasp and that you can achieve within a short time. The clearance method that I'm going to teach you in this book is super simple and it's quick to use. This means that you can start seeing results quickly.

Here's what one of my pregnant mamas says about using the head trash clearance method:

> "What's even better is that I didn't have to set aside hours upon hours to work through my fears. When a fear popped up during my pregnancy, I spent about 5-10 mins using the head trash clearance method and the fear was gone. It was incredibly empowering to know I could successfully rid myself of a fear in such a short period of time."

I promise that if you follow the how-to guide that I'm going to share with you in this book, that you'll notice a difference in your head space. How much will depend on how much clearance work you do, but you will. However, it's going to take more than simply reading this book. You'll have to step up and do the work. If you're up for that, then, what are we waiting for? Let's go! There's no time to lose. How much longer are you going to carry all this head trash through life; it's exhausting! It's stopping you from being YOU. It's holding you back from living your best life. How much longer can you wait? It's time to let it go and experience the life you were meant to enjoy. The head trash clearance method that I'm going to share with you has been proven to change lives, and there's no reason it can't change yours. Are you ready?

ONE

What's Head Trash?

I f I'm going to share with you how you can go about clearing your head trash, an obvious place to start would be to get clear on what head trash is.

Head trash includes all those thoughts, feelings, and emotions that take up head space that you'd rather do without. They're your anxieties, stresses, worries, concerns, and fears. They're your persistent negative emotions that weigh you down and cloud your thinking. Those negative thoughts and feelings affect your behaviour in ways you don't like or might not even be aware of. If you're the kind of person who likes lists, then this next bit is for you. Head trash includes things like...

- The little voice in your head that won't shut up and always churns out negative chatter
- Big scary images in your head that show you the worst possible outcome for something, thereby preventing you from doing it or doing it well
- Limiting thoughts and beliefs about yourself that hold you back

- Fears and phobias that prevent you from doing and enjoying things
- Self-sabotaging thoughts and patterns of behaviours that turn you into your own worst enemy
- Emotions that you carry inside you ALL the time that are just not helpful. Emotions like fear, anger, guilt, sadness, frustration, etc.
- Emotions that you display inappropriately, either excessively or consistently

Phew! That sounds like a lot! And for some people it IS a lot. Their heads are full of this crap. And it drives them, and the people around them, completely crazy. If only they could get rid of it. If this sounds familiar then you can stop worrying. You're in the right place, because that's what this book is about. Getting rid of your head trash so that you create more head space and find some bloody peace. Yee haah!

One day, someone asked me to come up with a definition of head trash and this is what I came up with:

Head trash [*noun*]: the accumulated subconscious patterns of thought and behaviour that prevent you from being awesome.

When I first came across the therapy that inspired the technique that I'm going to be sharing with you, I was blown away. At that point in my life, my head was bloody mess. I had spent the best part of my twenties desperately searching for my purpose and my reason for being here. Career-wise, I was doing pretty well; unfortunately, I was doing pretty well in jobs that left me feeling unfulfilled, and that's nothing to write home about, believe me.

I had this really strong sense that I was meant to "do something" during my stint here on planet Earth but I just didn't know what. As a result of this kind of thinking, I just felt out of place where I was. It felt wrong. It all felt very temporary, as though I were waiting for something. I just didn't know what. This started to become quite a drag, I can tell you. I searched high and low for the answer. I went to Tony Robbins's events and got sucked into his whole universe for a while (he does that to you). I did Reiki. I studied Buddhism and got into meditation. I went to palm-readers and mediums. I thought that maybe I could find it in *The Secret* or the Law of Attraction, I even read John Assaraf's *The Answer*, but I still didn't find the bloody answer. Against this murky backdrop, the time-space continuum of my life got ripped apart.

One rainy September day, I found out that my mum had cancer. She had cancer when I was teenager, but she had everything removed and we thought it had gone. Well it hadn't. Immediately, we brought her back from Paris where she has been staying with my aunt and my grandmother to have more tests. The day she arrived at the hospital, she collapsed. What followed were scans and more tests and then we found out that she had nine tumours in her brain. Six weeks later, she was gone. Just like that. I was thirty and devastated.

What followed would be the darkest period of my life. For the year that followed, I was a grief-stricken mess and could mostly be found sobbing in the foetal position. What I didn't realise at the time was that my mother and I had a relationship that wasn't the typical mother-daughter one. My parents divorced when I was four, so I ended up being her friend and partner. She turned to me for help in making our life and household decisions; where to go on holiday, what colour to paint the lounge, whether we should move back to France and be close to her family (like an idiot, I said no).

All this meant that the space in my heart allocated to "mother love" was bigger than it should have been and was taking up the space that we usually allocate for our significant other. In psychological terms, this is known as enmeshing. It means that when I lost her, a huge part of me left with her. I was left with a huge gaping hole and I lost all sense of who I was and why I was here. I was already struggling with the "why" question, but this took things to a whole new level. If you had asked me anything during that period, I would have answered with "I don't know"... Because I didn't. I just didn't know anything anymore.

The confident person who not long before had had a pretty successful marketing career now didn't know anything, and what little confidence I had was no more. I was a mess. I realised how much of a mess I was when I had to take my holiday allowance before I'd lose it. I had two weeks to take, which was pretty decent, and I could go somewhere nice. But I didn't want to go anywhere. I realised that no matter where I went, I'd be stuck with me; and I was the friggin' problem. I didn't want to go on holiday with me.

This was serious. I LOVE travelling, yet here I was, deciding that I didn't want to go. At that time in my life, I felt that I had limited options. I was either going to turn to drink and drugs just so that I could hide and forget what I was feeling, or I was going to have to sort this out. But this would require some bloody miracle to sort out. When you're a mess like that, it's not obvious what to do. I can see why people get stuck in these crappy places; they just don't know what the hell to do about it.

I had just read *Eat, Pray, Love* by Elizabeth Gilbert and I knew that I needed a bit of what she got when she had stayed in an ashram in India. I needed to be locked in a cave with my demons so that I could face them and put them to rest. But two weeks isn't enough time to travel to India from the UK and then trek across India get to an ashram and stay long enough for it to make any difference. I looked into retreats, but they weren't hardcore enough. Daily yoga and green juices weren't going to sort my mess out.

Then I discovered *The Hoffman Process* and thought I had struck gold. The Hoffman Process is a residential therapeutic retreat where, over the period of eight days, they break you down and show you what you're made of. It sounded a little brutal at times, but it was just what I needed. Doing Hoffman saved me. The thing is, having your crappy bits removed is all very good, but then all I was left with was a bare shell. I needed to start building again. So I wasn't out of the woods by any means. But I knew I was out of the quagmire and onto dry land, and that was a huge improvement.

Around this time, I came across this new therapy I mentioned earlier. Forgive me for taking you on a brief tour of the train wreck that was my emotional life, but I think it was important to give some context. When I said earlier that when I tried this new therapy and was "blown away," perhaps you can now get a sense of what that meant to me. I wasn't new to this head-sorting business. I had a whole wardrobe of t-shirts for various head-sorting things. I had tried a boatload of techniques, philosophies, and therapies, so I said I was blown away because not only was it working but also I was noticing a HUGE shift in how I was feeling... for the first time in a very, very, very long time.

Let's say you've got an old musty chair that you want to get rid of. So you throw it in the trash. Now it's gone. The space where the chair was is now clear. You can't smell it anymore, there are no bits of broken chair on the floor, and the cushion isn't hiding in a corner; the chair is just gone. Well that's what doing work with this therapy was like. One minute my head trash was there, then we'd clear it, and then it was gone without a trace. This feeling inspired the term *head trash* for me and *head trash clearance*. That's how it felt! Don't get me wrong. I'm not laying claim to that term; it just felt like a perfect way to describe my experience.

The more I used this term the more I liked it. It seemed so perfect to describe the crap we have in our heads. What's great about it is that it's a neutral term. When you imagine someone going to therapy or counselling, one of the first things the therapist is likely to ask is, "What's the problem or issue you want help with?" The words *problem* and *issue* are inherently loaded with negativity. They sound like bad things to have, things to be ashamed of.

Well, head trash isn't that. We all have it and it's nothing to be ashamed of. Are you ashamed of the rubbish in your bin at home? No! Your rubbish at home is something that you used to have a need for but now you no longer have a requirement for it. The packaging was useful while you brought the food home from the shop, but now that you've eaten it, you don't need it. The trousers you bought because you loved the colour are now being thrown because they don't fit so well. Are you ashamed of them? No. They're simply surplus to requirements. Just like your head trash.

At one point in your life, it served you well to be selfish because perhaps you were one of seven kids, and, if you weren't selfish, you never got anything. But maybe now you need to let go of some of your selfishness because you're bringing more of it to the table than you need to; it's excess to requirements. You're the breadwinner and have a family to think about. Your being super selfish is no longer required.

So we simply need to clear the excess selfishness and bring you back in balance. Selfishness does have good and bad aspects, as does everything. Nothing is totally good or bad, but there's good and bad in everything. Let's take water, for example. Too little of it, we die, and too much of it, we die. We need balance. The same applies here. You need to be selfish and put yourself first... to a degree. Self-care is important. On a plane, we're encouraged to be selfish and put our mask on first before we can help others. The same is true in life. If you don't put yourself first, then you can't support others. However, if you put your needs first ALL THE BLOODY TIME, then you're taking things too far; you're not in balance.

So far, you might be reading this and thinking, *That's great Lex! I KNOW I have all this head trash, but how on earth do I just get rid of it?* Well, that's what this book is all about.

Over the course of this book, I'll share with you how you can identify what your head trash is and then how to clear it. In clearing your head trash, you'll free up your head space and find it much easier to remain calm and think clearly. This can lead to better decisions, better relationships, better sleep, more clarity, less stuck-ness, better sex, more focus, less procrastination... you name it! You up for that?

Great! But before we start, we just have to do this one little piece of house-keeping.

Start a Head Trash Clearance To-do List

The first thing I'd recommend is that you start a head trash clearance to-do list! We have to-do lists for everything else in our lives, yet we neglect to have a to-do list for clearing up our own mind and head space. We have shopping lists, work project lists, household chores list, yet the part of us that's the most important in ALL of this is our minds. If we're stressed, depressed, over-whelmed, or panicky, it doesn't really matter that we know where we are with our household chores, because inside we're a mess. If there's total mayhem inside our heads, surely that's the place to start, not that pile of crap that's built up near the back door. After all, we take our heads everywhere with us and it's with us until the end. Shouldn't that be the first place we start in terms of to-do lists? But we don't.

So why don't we have a head trash clearance to do list?

I guess one of the reasons for this is that we're not really sure how to tick things off such a list. What's the point in creating a list that's just going to get longer and longer, right? Well, not anymore! In this book, you have the secret recipe for ticking things off such a list, so now it makes total sense. Not only can you HAVE a head trash clearance to-do list, but also you can TICK THINGS OFF IT! Hallelujah!

Identify somewhere for you to capture your head trash clearance to-do-list. Here are some ideas;

- Notes app on your phone
- Evernote app

- A notebook - the kind that's made out of paper

I would even be so bold as to suggest that you dedicate a whole notebook to this. This is not because I think you're completely screwed and are a lost cause of head trashy proportions. Well, you might be; who knows? The reasons for the suggestion will become apparent later, but I wanted to mention it in case you have the perfect notebook lying around just waiting for its purpose to reveal itself.

As an aside, dedicating a whole notebook to this is making a pretty powerful statement of intent. If I were you, I'd be getting the notebook sorted.

TWO

The Tell Tale Signs of Head Trash

W hen people ask what I do - depending on who it is and where I am - I might say, "I clear head trash." Incredibly, some people respond to that with, "Oh I don't think I have any." Ha! I used to cough my drink up at this point, but I've now learned to control myself.

Most people respond with, "Oh my God! I've got that!" The truth is we've all got head trash. Even me! Yes! Sure, I've been clearing head trash for a long time, but I had boatloads, and, in any case, this kind of work never ends. As long as you continue to live and interact with the world, you'll have experiences that can lead to a buildup of head trash, so it's just one of those things you need to keep on top of. You'd never hear someone say, "I don't have any house rubbish anymore - I don't use bins because I don't need them." Of course, you wouldn't. When you have a big clear-out at home, you don't think, "Oh great! That's me done. I'm never going to need to have a clear-out EVER AGAIN." Of course not. We just know that as long as we continue to buy and consume, we'll always need to throw stuff out. The same goes for our head space. It will always need a clear out.

Hopefully, by now, you're open to the possibility that you

might indeed have some head trash, but if you're still a bit sceptical, then let me share with you some of the telltale signs of head trash.

Voices in Your Head

Yes, I'm starting with the bleeding obvious. But I'm not talking about the crazy voices; this isn't that kind of book. I'm talking about the constant chatter going on. You debate with yourself endlessly as you ponder decisions and faff indecisively. Perhaps you keep replaying past conversations that didn't go the way you wanted them to. You narrate to yourself throughout the day, but not in a good way. Maybe you keep hearing your mother's voice as she berates you - yet again - or maybe you can't stop hearing that thing your dad always said to you as child.

These voices and conversations can intrude from all times and places into your mind, and to have it happen on some level is totally okay. But if you find yourself replaying a conversation from last Thursday about something that really doesn't warrant further thought, then something is amiss. An inability to let things go in this way is a classic sign of head trash.

Other People Annoy You ALL THE TIME!

The problem with living on an overpopulated planet is that there are people everywhere. And the more there are, the more annoying they become; at least they do if you have head trash. If you find that other people are always annoying you for some reason or another, then you've got some work to do, my friend. Sorry to break it to you like this, but it's true. They're pushing your buttons. It's okay.

We all have buttons that can be pushed, but the more you get annoyed, the more buttons you have... and a bucketful of buttons equals a bucketful of head trash. Lots of little opportunities to get you going. The solution here is to get rid of your buttons (and not depopulate the planet as some Bond baddies would like to do).

You Have Unhealthy Habits

You frequently indulge in activities and behaviours that are just not good for you. What I'm not referring to here are those times when we just kick back, let go, and indulge in some FUN. We all need to find a way to do that; life is about balance after all.

What I'm referring to here is when your life is mostly made up of these habits and the scales are tipping one way. So you drink regularly, perhaps daily (maybe 5 p.m. signals "happy hour" for you). You eat more than you need to, and you know this because you're overweight. You don't do any exercise. You smoke. You have addictions: maybe recreational drugs or prescription drugs and gambling. You spend hours and hours in front of screens: playing games, social media, checking the web, uploading selfies, playing candy crush, seeking likes to your posts, whatever. We know how bad screen time is; it's now considered a behavioural addiction. If technology takes up a high proportion on your non-work time then something's wrong here. Excessive shopping and spending are also included here.

Basically, anything that's not good for you. All of these behaviours are symptomatic of some disruption to the mind force and suggest some digging to understand why.

You're Stuck In Your Thinking

This is primarily in thought and behaviour. This is when you have to do things a certain way, perhaps you have a routine or "way" of doing something that you're pretty fixed on, and if an alternative way of proceeding is suggested or forced upon you, then you struggle. You resist, perhaps getting a bit sulky or difficult, or maybe you find that you simply can't do it. You're rigid in your thinking and you lack the flexibility in thought and behaviour to respond differently. I'm not referring to activities that have to be done in certain way or they don't work - like recipes or scientific experiments. This is more for things that really could be done in any number of ways. There's no difference really to the end result; it's more about how the journey makes you feel.

What I'm referring to here are your behaviours that other people might describe as a bit anal, or they might consider that you have a glimmer of OCD going on. When you get to do things your way, all is well with the world, but if something gets in your way, then you might become impatient, curt, rude, short-tempered, or just sulky and silent. These are all examples of emotions being triggered by head trash.

You Have Sleep Problems

Sleep issues are very common. I'm sure you've experienced some nights when you've struggled to fall asleep, or perhaps you've woken up in the middle of the night or early morning and couldn't get back to sleep. Most people experience this at some point or other, especially if life is a bit stressful (BIG clue right there!) The thing is, it's slightly different when insomnia is a regular fixture in your life, then it would be fair to say that there is some underlying issue that needs to be explored. There could be a nutritional angle, but, more than likely, there's a head trash angle too.

You're Easily Riled

You know how some people get irritated by the slightest thing. Minor events and occurrences just get them going. Maybe the motorway traffic is getting slow and they can't take it, so impatiently they decide to get off at the next exit and find another route, knowing that it's not really going to save them time. Or perhaps they're listening to a conversation, either among friends or on TV, that pushes their buttons and they react with strong emotion. They can't let it pass. Or maybe, if they're doing something around the house, say cooking or gardening and something gets knocked over or they drop something, then they react strongly, perhaps swearing or shouting to the thing that fell.

These are all small things that one could simply accept and let pass, but when there's head trash swirling round, then it triggers an outburst.

You Have Emotional Outbursts All The Time

And when you do, you always come out worse for them. You hate yourself for your reaction. You can almost see it coming, yet you can't help yourself and it backfires. This always reminds me of Wile E. Coyote from the old cartoons, trying to blow up the Road Runner, and all that ever happens is that he blows his own face off. We all get sucked in by emotional outbursts, but if they happen A LOT, then this is a sign that something's up.

Not being able to manage our emotions is a classic telltale sign of emotional imbalance due to too much head trash and is probably one of the best reasons to get cracking.

You Self-Sabotage

Yup! You get in your own way. You do it even when you know you're doing it, but you can't help yourself. Or maybe you don't even know you're doing it. Whichever it is, the things you want in life elude you and when you look back to try and understand why, you realise that the common thread is YOU! I'm sure you've heard of the Law of Attraction; well it has an opposite too - the Law of Repulsion - and that's what you've got going on.

Your Life Is Like *Groundhog Day*

For some reason, your life is stuck in a loop, and you keep playing reruns of the same soap opera life episodes as you repeat questionable patterns of behaviour. Do you always find yourself in the same crappy relationships or the same terrible life situations? Are there frustrating life patterns that keep cropping up for you? You might even feel like you're attracting them, and, on some level, you are... and yes it's that pesky head trash that's doing it! This is the Law of Attraction firing in the wrong direction.

You Struggle With Food, Drink or Drugs

You eat too much, you diet too much, you drink too much, you eat when you're sad, you drink when you're sad, or you drink when you celebrate. Don't get me wrong, drinking when you celebrate isn't always bad, except if for you *celebrate* means "I've made it through another kids' bedtime." or "Thank the lord! I've survived another day/week at work." Food and drink fill emotional gaps very well in ways we may not always realise. We don't really need to eat the quantities that we do, and if you find that you punctuate your day or week with a cheeky drink or comfort food, then you can be sure there's some head trash lurking nearby. If you're not sure, just look in the mirror. Not wanting to eat is also one to look out for, so obsessive dieting or food restriction. If you're over or underweight for your height, then this is most definitely a yes for you.

Illness Is Never Far Away

If you're regularly ill and pick up everything that's going round, then it's fair to say that your body is under stress and struggling to fight off infection. If your body is under stress, then the mind will be too. The body is a reflection of your mental and emotional space, so if your body is full of aches and pains or you're regularly popping pills for something then there's a head trash component that needs checking out.

You've Got An Emotional Stalker

Some people do a very good job at dragging negative emotional states around with them everywhere they go. Perhaps they're followed by the SAME emotion ALL THE TIME. Maybe it's stress, impatience, frustration, or anxiety. No matter what's happening or who they're with, they're frustrated: frustrated that they missed the train, frustrated that the person in front of them is taking ages finding the right money, frustrated that they can't find a parking spot. Even when they're out with their family having a pleasant day out, the invisible unwanted guest will be there. Now, I'm sure you know someone like this; we all do, but are YOU like this? If you find that you're leaping to your own defence and citing lots of reasons why you behave like this, then you're definitely guilty of having some emotional hanger-ons.

This little list is just for starters so if you read this and think "Nope... Not me.... I don't have that..." Then there are a couple of possibilities;

You're in denial

Yup! Sorry to be blunt, but I'm afraid this is a big possibility for you. You're doing a fantastic self-sabotaging job and persuading yourself that you don't actually have anything to work on. I've seen this before; in fact, I've got the T-shirt myself somewhere! And, on some level, you're right. You think you're fine... and on some level you are... you're happy with how you are. BUT and this is a BIG but, you lack the self-awareness that would help you to see that maybe, just maybe, you have some work to do.

If you're content, calm, and not really affected negatively by all the happenings of life around you, then you probably don't need to do this. But if you're stressed; struggle with confidence or self-esteem; procrastinate; avoid people, places, or actions for some reason; have trouble sleeping, eat or drink too much; have health issues; live day-to-day with things like guilt, anger, or resentment.... well, you get the picture!

All this stuff is a sign that you have things that need attention. So if this is you, then you might need to have a word with yourself because you're probably in denial on some level.

You're sorted!

You've spent the best part of your life in a cave meditating on the meaning of life and you've made it. You float about on your carpet of white light and nothing ever disrupts your calm happiness. You're an enlightened being who emanates peace and love. You're never stressed and never have a bad word to say about anything or anyone. In fact, people are drawn to you for your calming presence and your wise words. Yay for you! (Why did you pick up this book?)

THREE

Kat's Head Trash Clearance Story

I want to share with you a story about my friend Kat because, quite simply, it's a great head trash clearance story. Not only does it have a super impressive clearance reaction, but it also shows the link between mind and body.

Kat had popped round to say hello and we were perched on stools having coffee in my kitchen. At one point, I watched curiously as she bent over and appeared to be struggling with something. I asked what she was doing, because it wasn't very obvious. She told me that she was trying to yawn. Trying to yawn? Really? Since when is yawning such an effort? I had to ask! Kat went on to tell me that she hadn't yawned in weeks; she just couldn't. Wow! I'd never heard of that before. Immediately my head trash radar pricked up, so I began prodding. This is what she told me;

"Following a minor sports injury my breathing became heavy and I felt a constant weight in my chest, and often I struggled to get a sentence out without having to consciously pause to take a deep breath. My doctor told me it was stress, but the funny thing was, I felt fine. I've been a lot more distressed in my life, been through some pretty rubbish times, but now I was really happy and felt lucky to be me... I just struggled to breathe!

My injury healed and I got back in my running shoes, but the breathing problem persisted. I changed doctors and went through a series of tests - blood tests, lung tests, x-rays, ECGs and so on - all of which told me how wonderfully healthy my body is! I could only conclude that it was psychological, and began to recognise that although I felt grateful for what life brings me, I was very frustrated in a lot of areas of my life.

My work, which I'm very passionate about, is often held up by bureaucracy, I had recently had my values challenged by friends letting me down, and I felt a certain inertia in my life. All of this frustration was covered up by a perhaps 'British' sensibility of being firmly grateful for all the things I am lucky enough to have, and not wanting to complain, or ask for what I really want on top of all that."

At this point, my head trash alarm bells were well activated and I offered to help. Deep down, I just knew that her health challenges were from her feelings of frustration. I didn't say this, though, because, well, who on earth was I to think that I could help where the doctors had failed? (That's my imposter syndrome head trash, by the way).

Kat accepted my offer, so we moved to the lounge and I went into therapist mode. Over the next couple of hours, I worked with her using the method I'm going to be sharing with you later. We worked on her feelings of frustration because, let's face it, this was a common theme.

Here's how Kat describes her clearance experience;

"My session with Alexia is difficult to describe because it covered so much in just a couple of hours. I was asked to connect with my feelings of frustration, and, though this wasn't particularly hard, I found it got easier during the early part of the session... because I felt that nothing was happening. I felt that I should be feeling something, doing something, and anxious that I wasn't doing it right and was letting Alexia down! Her professional manner made me able to tell her this, and her sincere reassurance and patience made it possible for me to be totally open with her, which, as it turned out, I couldn't have been anything but."

Kat became very frustrated early on in the session. As she said, she felt she should have been feeling something or doing something. This was her frustration coming out. You can't clear on anything and not have it come to the surface!

"We went through a series of exercises, and, at each stage, she would ask me if I felt any changes. Gradually, at key words or phrases, I felt a shift, often a chill washing through my body (despite being under two thick blankets). These intensified over the session, until I had what I can only describe as a truly profound experience."

This was the moment in the session when the frustration that had become trapped in her system, released itself.

"An unstoppable wave of intense emotion came over me and my breathing suddenly became HUGE! It was as if my lungs were making up for six months of not being able to breathe - my chest felt like it was reaching for the ceiling! All the weight I felt in my chest was pushed out, and I was drawing in great volumes of air as my whole body became suddenly really hot."

At this point in the session, my jaw dropped to the floor. It was quite a sight. Kat had been lying down on my sofa and she suddenly sat up gulping in huge, deep breaths. It was like she had been kept underwater for a few minutes and has just re-surfaced and needed to replenish her oxygen. It was pretty epic and it went on for what felt like ages, but that's not all...

"Other things then began to happen - my head started to ache at specific points, which we then addressed directly to find their cause. I was totally astounded at the symbolism that my mind came up with: a skull, a duck, a gate, the letter A. Each one seemed so random at first, but then, because of my story and my life experiences, each gave total clarity on a different aspect of my frustration. Things I had never said out loud or admitted to myself before came out, and each time I felt a release of energy. And as Alexia dealt with it, in her incredibly compassionate and nurturing way, another chill, another change made.

"If nothing else, the session made me laugh at all the time I have spent trying to find explanations and meaning to my breathing problems, while the answer was there within me just waiting to have its voice and be listened to."

I love this. This is EXACTLY what I mean when I say that our truth is inside, just waiting to be heard; we just need to clear all the crap out the way so that we can tune into it.

"A few days on, and I am still seeing the shifts. I am still yawning: learning how to yawn again! It feels incredible to be able to do something so simple that I haven't been able to do for months. The weight in my chest simply isn't there anymore; my lungs still feel huge and healthy.

"I seem unable to really get het up about the things I used to - I feel far more serene. It's not that I feel spaced out; more that I'm able to be 'in the moment' yet somehow be more objective at the same time.

"I keep waking up earlier than usual, without an alarm, but not tired, and not full of energy, just awake. I listened patiently and attentively through a whole conference at work when normally at these events I'd be dreaming or scheming or planning something else at the same time as half-listening. My energy is more consistent throughout the day.

"Time seems to have slowed, in that before I was **always** rushing and late. I've been early or bang on time for every single thing I've done this week, and I've not rushed for anything. There just seems to be more time, which is very strange to me, but wonderful.

"I can't thank Alexia enough for the profound changes I've experienced during and since my session. It's given me a renewed respect for my own mind and body, and I'll make sure I listen much better to myself in future. It's a session I couldn't recommend enough - if you want true lasting change in your life, then this is the way to make it."

Over the course of this book, I'm going to share with you what I did so that you too can do the same.

By the time you finish reading this book, you'll know how to clear this stuff from your life.

Are you up for that?

FOUR

The Head Trash Clearance Journey

This is the bit in the book where I give you a sneaky overview of what lies ahead on your head trash clearance journey. I don't know about you, but when I head off somewhere, I'm not just interested in the destination, I'm pretty curious about the bit in between; the journey that's going to get me there. And while I'm at it, I'll give you a glimpse of what's waiting for you at the destination; the light that's waiting for you at the end of the tunnel should you wish to embark on this head trash clearance journey.

The Head Trash Clearance Path to En-lighten-ment

What's there to gain from doing head trash clearance? Well, I could dive into specifics, but I'll save that for later. In a nutshell? En-lighten-ment. I'm not talking about the spiritual term, although, to be honest, this is a very spiritual path. And by *spiritual* I want to highlight an important aspect of being spiritual, which is "becoming a better version of who you are." So when I talk about en-lighten-ment I mean, lightening up and letting go of all the stuff that takes you away from being the real you. The awesome, incredible you who lives inside and who's yearning to be heard and seen, and desperate to get out and to shine. It's very possible that your inner light is being blocked by all your "stuff": your fears, anxieties, stresses, your head trash!

I'm a firm believer that the person deep inside of all of us, knows what to do. You *know* what makes you happy and what you should be doing with your life. You *know* what decisions to make. You *know* the direction you need to head in. You just KNOW. When I was in my lost phase, I was the total opposite to this. I didn't know anything.

Many people are in this lost place. They don't know either, because they can't connect to their heart and their intuition. The fears, stresses, and anxieties are shouting so loud in their heads that they can't hear the whisper of the heart. So, when you lighten the load and let go of all this stuff, you start to become you. The real you. And without wanting to get all hippy on you, but I'm going to: this is where you find inner peace and contentment. The holy friggin grail, right?

So this enlightenment that I'm talking about is when you lighten up. You become the light. The way forward is lit and clear for you; you can see a path. Oh, and there is a path.

Would you like to know where you are on this path? Because there is a path, and it has key stages, at least it does for me.

I think a good place to start would be at the beginning; the start of the head trash clearance journey.

People at the very beginning of the head trash path to en-lighten-ment can be best described as prickly. Prickly just like a chestnut shell - you know the spiky husk they grow in. They're a bit like the ones you get for playing conkers but they have loads more spikes. They're almost thistle like. If I asked you to pick one of these things up, how would you feel about that? You'd probably shy away. Perhaps you'd put some gloves on. Not only to protect you from the prickliness but also because the prickles are delicate.

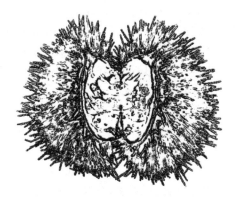

People with a lot of head trash are like chestnuts. They're prickly customers who need to be handled with care, maybe even with kid gloves. They get trodden on or feel trodden on.

In fact, they often feel like the victim in whatever scenario they find themselves in. Victims tend to feel powerless and believe that the solution to their ills lies elsewhere. They don't tend to take responsibility for their problems because they feel that these terrible things have simply happened to them. They simply don't see that maybe they might have had a role to play somewhere along the line. I hate to say it, but they can be a bit toxic and leave a mark. They're often hurtful and cause pain in their behaviours, although not necessarily deliberately.

These prickly people tend to affect those around them in negative ways; if you get too close, you'll more than likely get hurt. At the very least, you'll come away feeling the pang of a prick. These poor folk will get sucked into whatever drama is around them. Imagine running a chestnut along a dusty floor or a wooly jumper. It's pretty much guaranteed that the chestnut will pick up a load of fluff and rubbish. If you keep doing that, the chestnut will eventually have all sorts of nonsense stuck to it, just like people have. Their stuff might be unhealthy relationships, bad habits, other people's dramas, destructive behaviours, and huge doses of self-sabotage.

Depending on how long the person has been like this, eventually, the weight of their head trash is going to start affecting their body. They might start having problem skin or hair. Digestive issues or irritable bowel syndrome (IBS) might start creeping in, as might restless or sleepless nights. If any of these are left unchecked, it can lead to all sorts of physical ailments. The dis-ease in our emotions is what leads to disease in the body, and often the person who is ill all the time, has a bunch of inner work to do.

Please don't think I'm having a go at these people at this stage; I'm not. I used to be one! I think it's important to get a sense of what it looks like to be overcome with head trash. Perhaps you recognise some of this in yourself or in the people around you.

If such a person were to start undertaking head trash clearance, their next evolution would be the washing machine ball. You know those plastic balls some people put in their washing machines? These people still have spikes, but they've been reduced in number and they're nowhere near as prickly. People like this start to feel much stronger in themselves, especially compared to where they were. This is all relative, remember; it's a journey. But, just like a washing ball, they feel tossed about by life. They're not really in control of things; things control them. Often, it can feel like they're going round in circles because they are!

They still have a lot of internal conflicts pulling in several different directions, and it's spinning them out a bit. One minute, they're doing this, and the next, they try that; they struggle to focus. Their self-sabotage is actually making them go round in circles. Perhaps they keep being attracted to the same crappy relationships, or maybe they keep making the same mistakes. They know they're doing it, but they can't seem to stop. This is because deep conflicts need to be resolved, and until they are, they all continue to self-sabotage and go round and round. They also tend to find it hard to stick to something long enough to make a difference, so they give up and ping right back to where they were. Yo-yo dieting is a classic example of head trash needing to be cleared. So what's next?

Well, let's say our washing ball continues on their head trash clearance journey. What delights await them? They become a bouncy ball! You know, those rubber bouncy balls that kids love! Now is when life can start to feel a bit more fun. Who doesn't want a bouncy ball in their lives? Washing balls? No thanks! But bouncy ball? Hell, yes! The prickly bits have been dealt with. People now positively enjoy your presence. But it's not all roses.

You're a bit unpredictable. People aren't quite sure how you're going to react; you're a bit inconsistent. One minute you're on top of the world and all smiles, then, suddenly, you hit a low. If you're not careful, you find that you go off the rails pretty easily, which annoys you as much as it annoys those around you.

Unfortunately, you still have the potential to rub others the wrong way. Other people's energy and actions trigger you very easily. You're not what one could describe as "emotionally resilient." Little things still set you off. I think this is where most people are. The world is full of bouncy balls, and it can feel a bit hectic. But like the wonderful depiction of a world full of bouncy balls from the Sony Bravia advert from the noughties, it's also beautiful. It's people's quirks and foibles that make life interesting and colourful. The best music comes from troubled souls and people wrestling with their stuff. This isn't, by any means, a bad place to be. Hell, I spent years there!

When I share this with you, let me be clear, there is no judgement with any of these stages. There is no good or bad stage to be at. They just are. They each have positive and negative aspects, and they're each loaded with opportunities for learning and growth. Whether you're open to it or choose to take action is something else. Anyway, what's next? If you choose to continue with your head trash clearance, what's your next incarnation? Can you guess?

It's a snooker ball! You're less of a lightweight now, and you're more grounded. You've got more of a solid vibe about you. People take great pleasure from simply being with you. Who doesn't like holding a snooker ball in their hand? The shininess, the weight, the heaviness, the coolness to the touch; all of it feels so good. As a package, it works. But, as with a snooker ball, you get a bit of a buffeting.

Now that you're stronger, people who aren't as strong as you are drawn to you. Consequently, you get poked and pushed around a bit. People come to you for help with their dramas, and, because you're still a work-in-progress in terms of your own inner emotional life, you get easily sucked into the pockets of their lives. You want to help them and feel like you have the energy and ability to help them, so you try. But you quickly get frustrated because, all too often, your help doesn't seem to make too much of a difference, and it drains you.

As a snooker ball, you have much more focus in your life; if you were feeling stuck in life before, now you're starting to get unstuck and feel like you have a clear direction or aim. At times, you make incredible progress and score some wins, but then, out of nowhere, you get knocked into darkness and wonder what the hell happened. You've hit one of your big blocks, that's what! The closer we get to succeeding and fulfilling our destiny, the more we get tested. At times like this, our resolve is tested - do we really want this? We have to dig deep to get ourselves back up.

Many people struggle to pick themselves up and get back on track. It's not always easy. It takes more mindset work, more inner work, more head trash clearance, but those who do the work can succeed. And what's waiting for them is the light at the end of tunnel. The light that signals en-lighten-ment. So what is it? What ball do you become as you reach enlightenment? Well, it's the best ball there is! A glitter ball!

Who doesn't want to be a glitter ball? The glitter ball is the life and soul of the party.

As a glitter ball, you notice that you're able to rise above the drudgery of day-to-day life. You have a new perspective and things just don't seem to affect you in the same way. There's a bit more distance and things just feel more peaceful, somehow.

As a glitter ball, people are drawn to your energy, charisma, cheeriness, and calmness. You're like a beacon in the sea of emotional chaos.

It might seem as though people are drawn to you because of your brightness and your light. But the truth is that it isn't your light they're seeing; it's theirs. You help them to find the light that exists within them; you're simply reflecting their own brilliance back at them. You inspire them to be more. But don't be fooled. Your work isn't finished. You still have chinks that need work; this work will never end. But you're most definitely on the home stretch... in terms of head trash clearance anyhow.

Where are you on this journey to enlightenment?

FIVE

Why This Works When Other Techniques Struggle

You might be reading this as someone who's been on a head trash clearance mission for a while. You feel you've tried everything. Yet, you're still affected by stuff that has bothered you for years. If this is you, then I suspect, on some level, you might be reading this book with some mild suspicion. "Why would this succeed where others have failed?" What's so different that means it's actually going to work?

First, it's worth saying that some things work great for some people but not for others. Finding a technique or tool that works for everyone is impossible. Just as with medicine, some people respond and some don't. This is why I believe it's worth having a bunch of tools and techniques at your fingertips. That way, you can pick and choose, or mix and match until you get the desired result.

Thus, I believe that one of the reasons that the method I'm sharing with you in this book works so well, is that it tackles the hidden dimensions of your head trash that probably haven't been addressed before. The head trash clearance method is like the Heineken of clearance methods, it reaches the parts that other clearance techniques don't reach. And this can give you the results that have previously eluded you.

Think of your head like a large house that needs a big tidy-up and a massive clear-out; it's just cluttered with stuff everywhere you look. You decide that enough is enough and that it's time to have a clear-out. You start with the main rooms that you spend time in: the kitchen, the living room, and the bedroom. You tackle the surfaces with a big plastic bag, gathering heaps of stuff as you go.

After a day of bag-filling, the difference is amazing. You feel like you've done a great job, which is reaffirmed as you cast a glance over your new clear surfaces. Aah! You can breathe! Now, this might appear like a job well done, but unfortunately, you've only done a fraction of the job. Many other places still need to be cleared out. What about inside the drawers and the cupboards? What about the spare bedroom that's become a dumping ground? Or how about the attic or the garage, did you do that too? Did you tackle the food cupboards? And what about that set of drawers in the hall that seems to collect all the random items of the house? And let's not forget the cupboard under the stairs? Or the suitcases under the bed and on top of the wardrobe?

You see, when you think about it, there are lots of places that need a clear-out; your stuff is hiding in all sorts of places. Eventually, it will seep out and the surfaces will become cluttered once more. You've only scratched the surface.

The same goes for your head trash. Often when we tackle head trash, we go to the obvious places like the surfaces in our home, and when we notice a difference, we stop, thinking the job is done. But it's not; there's more. Our head trash is hiding in a lot more places, but because we haven't tackled those hiding places, then the head trash still affects us. It might take time for it to surface again, but, eventually, it does. This means that you might find yourself revisiting certain themes in your life repeatedly, thinking, *I thought I'd dealt with this already*. Our head trash will only be cleared once we clear it out of ALL its hiding places; otherwise, traces remain and the thing we want to be rid of is still there bothering us.

So what are these hidden places? I've called these the hidden dimensions of head trash.

SIX

The Hidden Dimensions of Head Trash

W hen we imagine a person in therapy, it's usually with one person on a couch talking about their problem and how it's affecting them. If their problem is negative, then the person on the couch is probably talking about how much they hate having this problem because of how much it's causing them upset in their life.

This all sounds fair enough, doesn't it? We could say that in this particular therapy session, the therapist is helping the person to explore one dimension on their problem, where it relates to themselves. In fact, they're only actually exploring half a dimension because it sounds like they're only talking about how much the person hates their problem.

Now already, we're stumbling into problems. If we only look at the aspects that we hate about this problem, we're missing half the picture. What about the aspects that we love? This might sound like an odd thing for me to suggest, but it's actually an important point that has been overlooked, and I'm going to talk more about this in a bit.

So yes, the first place we've been going wrong is not exploring those aspects of our problem that we love or are grateful for. We can't resolve a problem fully if we only look at one side of it. And we certainly can't let go of it fully if we only let go of half of it. If we want to clear our head trash around something, we need to clear out the love energy we have for it as well as the hate energy. But it doesn't stop there.

When we open our eyes to the vastness of our emotional landscape, it's quickly evident that we have much more baggage around an emotional issue than what we've been looking at up until now; how we as individuals negatively experience the problem. We're social creatures on an overpopulated planet; whatever personal emotional challenge we have doesn't only affect us, and it would be naive to think so. It affects other people too. And the bit that we've failed to explore is this: what happens to us when these other people are being affected by this thing? When you take a closer look, we get affected quite a lot actually. We don't operate in silos; we're very much interconnected with those around us, yet this is rarely explored in therapeutic terms when people are being supported in dealing with their emotional challenges. Let me explain.

Let's imagine that you're out with your partner having dinner in a nice restaurant. You've just finished your starter and you're enjoying the welcome pause that comes between dishes when you notice a couple at the next table. You notice them because of the way the husband is speaking to his wife; he seems to be incredibly rude and disrespectful, and is saying things to his wife that you find uncomfortable to listen to. You try to ignore it, but you're finding it quite hard because you're wondering how on earth she's putting up with it. Your mind wanders from the lovely conversation that you were having and you start imagining the things that you might like to say to put him in his place.

The man at the next table continues with his disrespectful ways but, this time, directing them to the waiter. On hearing how he speaks to the waiter, you can feel tension rising inside and you notice that you're starting to feel quite mad. More than anything, you want to jump to the defence of the wife or the waiter and put this man in his place. Your partner notices that you seem distracted but you shrug it off. But the thing is, you can't shrug it off. You're annoyed and as long as you continue listening to this man carry on like this, you get more and more annoyed and angry.

This has become *your* problem.

But why? This has nothing to do with you. The man is not directing any of his rudeness or his lack of respect to you. It's the wife's and the waiter's problem. So how come this has now become your problem? Hmmm. Does this situation sound familiar?

Have you ever found yourself wound up by other people's behaviour when you have no idea who they are and what they're doing has absolutely nothing to do with you? Well, my friend, you have just been triggered by one of the hidden dimensions of head trash!

These kinds of situations demonstrate there are other dimensions to our head trash that we need to take into consideration when doing emotional clearance work; focusing solely on how a problem affects us individually isn't enough. We also need to address other aspects to the problem, aspects that we may have previously dismissed. So what are these other hidden aspects?

Head trash has many dimensions, and, to be honest, I could write a book on just those, so I'm going to keep this short and focus on those dimensions that have the potential to have the greatest impact on the clearance work you do.

1. The head trash; the idea of it

This is the very idea of the head trash. It's not personal and doesn't relate to anyone specifically. It's merely the concept of something.

A great example here is Depression (I'm deliberately using a capital D here as I'm referring to the condition referred to as Depression, as opposed to occasional bouts of depressed feelings).

We hear Depression mentioned a lot in the context of mental health, and it frequently makes the news, often triggered by the revelations of yet another celebrity owning up to suffering from it or, sadly, choosing to end their life because of it. The ensuing discussions and debate might go on to talk about how little support is available for sufferers or how it's so often misunderstood.

When we hear Depression talked about in this way, it doesn't really have a personal angle; instead, it's being debated as a *thing*. Let's say that you suffer from Depression or that you occasionally experiences bouts of depressed feelings and you hear such a story come up on the news. How might that make you feel? It's highly probable that it would have an effect on you in some way. Maybe it would remind you of how you feel when you're depressed. Or perhaps you might feel a dark, empty feeling creep back in or be reminded of the times when you were depressed. Whatever your response, it's highly unlikely that you would hear a story of Depression on the news and not be affected in some way.

Compare that to a person who doesn't suffer from Depression who hears the same story. This person might not even notice the story when it comes on and they would simply carry on doing whatever it is they were doing as the news carries on in the background. For them, it's a non-event.

This is what we refer to as the first dimension of head trash, the very idea of it. We can't ignore the fact that simply hearing about something being discussed - depression, miscarriage, death, burglary, rape, etc. - can be a trigger to an internal response that might include sounds or images coming to mind or physical feelings or sensations in our body. This response could be mild or it might kick off a cascade of thoughts, feelings, and emotions that knock us for six.

When we're talking about this dimension of head trash, this is how we express it:

- Anger
- Depression, depressed feelings
- Pain

2. Your experience of it; you experiencing the head trash
This dimension of head trash is the one that we're most aware of and is the one that's usually tackled in many talking therapies: head trash and how we experience it.

From the examples I shared with you above, this dimension of head trash is expressed like this:

- Anger: me being angry, me experiencing anger
- Depression: me being / feeling depressed, me experiencing Depression / depressed feelings
- Pain: me being in pain, me experiencing pain

We're all too familiar exploring our feelings within this dimension, but perhaps the aspect that we don't consider enough, is how we might love this thing that bothers us. This might sound like an outlandish statement but, on some level, we need to acknowledge that a small part of us loves the thing that we hate. We might never want to admit this to ourselves, but we need to take a look nonetheless, particularly if we've had this problem for years. If we didn't love it so, we'd have gotten rid of it already.

Let's take the person who experiences bouts of depression, for example. When he's having a bad phase, he might be fortunate enough to have good friends and family who step in and help him take care of himself. Perhaps his family uses it as an excuse to visit and check up on him.

On some level, he'll love this degree of connection that depression brings him. Deep down, he might think if it weren't for his depressed phases, he might not see his friends and family as much; so why would he stop being like this? Thus, it would follow that, on some level, he loves it. That's not to say that any of this is conscious or deliberate, but if we're to truly let go of something, we need to recognise that a small part of us loves this thing too. Many people choose not to overcome a phobia or an emotional challenge, even though they can do so. Why would that be?

3. Other people being affected by the head trash

This is when other people are being affected by the head trash in question. These other people have nothing to do with you; they're just other folk who are also experiencing this emotional challenge.

So, working through our examples, this is how that might be expressed:

- Anger: other people being angry / experiencing anger
- Depression: other people being depressed, experiencing depression
- Pain: other people being in pain / experiencing pain

4. When you make other people experience the head trash

This is where things get interesting because, now, we start to acknowledge the role we play in making others experience head trash and how that, in turn, might affect you.

In terms of our examples, this is how it looks:

- Anger: me making other people experience anger, me angering others, me making other people feel angry
- Depression: me depressing others, me making other people feel depressed
- Pain: me making other people experience pain, me inflicting pain on other people

There are different levels and aspects within this dimension that are worth stating. After all, it's possible to make someone else experience something by accident or deliberately, just as it's possible to encourage or support them in experiencing something. Let me show you what I mean:

- Me deliberately making someone else angry - by knowingly damaging their property, by being rude to their face
- Me accidentally making someone else angry - by being late, by unwittingly saying something they don't agree with
- Me encouraging someone to stay angry - by reminding them of why they're angry and reinforcing their view, by saying something that I know will re-ignite their anger

All of these are examples of you making the other person experience it, but they are subtly different.

5. When other people or situations make you experience the head trash

Our final dimension is when other people (or situations) make you experience the head trash. In other words, this is when you're experiencing the feeling or displaying the behaviour because of someone or something. This dimension acknowledges those situations where we're actually being triggered by something:

- Anger: other people or situations making me angry, other people or situations angering me
- Depression: other people or situations making me feel depressed, other people or situations depressing me
- Pain: other people or situations making me feel/experience pain

In taking a closer look at this aspect, we're able to better understand how other people experiencing this thing also affects you. Thus, in the restaurant scenario I shared earlier, even though these other people (the wife and the waiter) were experiencing disrespect and rudeness, you were the one who was being triggered emotionally.

It's important for us to acknowledge how the world around us affects us, even though we might not be targeted directly. If we're to live a life that's as close to stress-free and calm as possible, it helps if we can free ourselves from the ways that other peoples' behaviour can affect and influence us, even though we're not being targeted directly with the behaviour.

Now I'm quite a visual person, so to help me get my head around all this when I was training, I created this little diagram. I've since found that the people who attend my trainings love this little picture too.

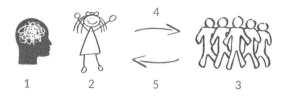

Where
1. The idea of it
2. You experiencing the head trash
3. Other people experiencing the head trash
4. You making others experience the head trash
5. Others making you experience the head trash

Even though I've just shared five dimensions of head trash with you, in this model, there are ten because each one is made up of two parts; the love aspect and the hate aspect. These dimensions show up in the head trash clearance method in the form of the head trash clearance mantras, which I'll be sharing with you later.

The head trash clearance mantras

Each head trash clearance mantra relates to one of the dimensions of head trash, so by working your way through each of the dimensions, you're in fact undertaking a very thorough emotional clear-out.

Not only that but it's a deep level of work that you wouldn't have done through traditional therapeutic means, simply because traditional talking therapies don't help you let go and clear the emotional baggage that's hiding in these other dimensions. In fact, most just work on what's hiding in half of one dimension, as I touched on at the beginning.

So, you could say that this approach has ten times the depth of clearance. Twenty times when you acknowledge the power that's contained in clearing the opposite too. Wowsers!

SEVEN

Where Does Our Head Trash
Come From?

I n my early days of learning about the workings of the mind, I
really wanted to get a sense of the overall picture of how
things worked. I had so many questions and I was seeking some
kind of structure to it all. The first thing I wanted to know was
where my head trash came from. My reasoning was that if I knew
where it came from, then surely I could stem the inward flow. Was
there even an inward flow? Is that how this stuff works? I had no
idea. So I started playing round with some ideas with one of my
early teachers and mentors, Chris Milbank. During his training
courses, he would often use the metaphor of lakes to describe the
accumulation of stress and the subsequent impact of allowing it to
build up.

Chris's lakes metaphor went like this: When you're stressed, if
left unchecked, the stress starts piling up. And, as we're talking
about lakes, then you start to fill up your lake of stress. As Lake
Stress fills up and starts to take shape, you start noticing the
impact of stress on your life: your hair, your skin, your sleep, your
health, your digestion. It all starts to reveal your inner stressed
state. If you continue to remain stressed and aren't taking any

stress-reduction measures, then, eventually, your lake starts to overflow and starts filling a new lake.

This new lake is Lake Anxiety. Whereas Lake Stress was kind of pretty as lakes go, Lake Anxiety looks a bit more threatening. It's got some dark deep patches that look like they might be hiding all sorts of horrid things. These could be things like your addictive habits, the panic attacks that start to creep in, and that constant murky feeling you have in the pit of your stomach.

If you continue to allow the stress to build up and the anxiety to be unchecked, then I'm sure you can guess what happens next. Lake Anxiety starts to overflow and a new lake is formed: Lake Depression. Lake Depression is what it sounds like, depressing. It will start as bouts of feeling low and depressed, but, if things continue, then it can become full-on Depression, which something we'd all like to avoid.

Now I think it's worth stating, at this point, that this is just a theory, but it's a theory Chris had put to the test quite a bit over the years. It informed the way he worked with his clients who were suffering from what he referred to as the Big Three: stress, anxiety, or depression. His solution was very simple: find the source of the stress and deal with it (i.e., stop it from being a source of stress.) This stops the inward flow, thus allowing the lakes to drain and the levels of depression, stress, and anxiety to be reduced.

When we talk about emotions and matters of the mind, it can all feel so nebulous that using metaphor or analogy can help us grasp some of the finer details. That's not to say that any metaphor we come up with is perfect; it's simply a way to help us to understand something. I certainly found the lakes metaphor very useful and was able to observe it in action on my own clearance journey.

When I first started clearing my head trash, I think I was flitting between anxiety and depression. As I began to identify those things in my life that were stressing me out and making me feel discomfort daily, I would work on them. The more I worked on them, the more I noticed that I was experiencing less depression and anxiety. I was still stressed, but it felt more manageable; things were changing! The thing is, I was curious and wanted to understand the bigger picture. What about my other head trashy bedfriends, like my limiting beliefs? Where were they in the grand scheme of things in relation to these lakes? Was there a link or a relationship somehow? I felt that there would be. My crappy beliefs about me and life were bound to be causing me stress. And what about my inner conflicts? Where did they fit in all of this? I really wanted to get a handle on this. When I finally started making great progress in sorting out the mess that was my head, I wanted to keep going, but I needed to know how to go about tackling all of this.

In the head trash clearance method, I knew I had a great tool for the job, but I just needed a roadmap or a plan of some sort so that I could crack on. That's probably my head trash and my silly need for structure, but I'm cool with that because it motivated me to search for answers.

I started to play around with some ideas, and because the idea of lakes was already firmly in my head, this was my starting point so I decided to expand the lakes metaphor to encompass the broader picture. The obvious next metaphor for me to latch onto was our old friend from geography lessons at primary school, the water cycle. Lakes fill with water from the sky, right? So this seemed to be a perfectly logical place to start. I began by drawing the classic water cycle diagram and thinking about the various elements and how they might represent elements or aspects of our head trash. Nature always has the answers, so I felt confident that I wouldn't be led astray if I proceeded down this route. Nature's patterns and behaviours are found at every scale, so, for all I knew, I might be onto something.

I spent quite a bit of time playing around with this and would often check in with my mentor Chris to see if what I was suggesting was making sense psychologically and therapeutically. After plenty of testing and observing, I eventually decided that the water cycle had merit in helping me to understand the nature of our head trash, and, more importantly, how to clear it. And if it helped me to better understand head space and how to clear it, then maybe it'll help you too.

Disclaimer: this is just my theory. It has not been put through any clinical research, and I've not tested it on rats or mice.

EIGHT

The Head Trash Cycle

W hen you think of a diagram of the water cycle, you imagine a snow-capped mountain, some lovely clouds, a bit of rain, and a nice river running down the mountain into the sea. Oh, and some arrows. Lot of arrows!

For me, the water running down the mountains into streams and then rivers and lakes are our emotions and the clouds represented our values and our beliefs. This is where it all starts. This is what feeds the rivers.

Now, let's imagine for a minute a nice sunny day with some white fluffy clouds gently scattered across the sky. Our fresh mountain stream is running clear and as it gets further down the mountain. It meets up with the water from other nearby streams and eventually becomes a river that meanders its way to the sea. Things are flowing beautifully and nature is thriving. This scene represents a healthy emotional landscape. But, we're never going to learn anything when things are going well, so let's mess things up a bit and see what happens. Let's start with the river.

When we think of rivers going BAD, there are a few things that could happen.

The first is that the river levels start rising. If this continues then it might lead to the flooding of the area beyond the river. This is a bit like our lakes metaphor from earlier. If you're overcome with too much emotion that you simply can't handle or that becomes too much for you, you become overwhelmed. Stress begins to build up when the river walls get breached. The capacity of the river, the strength of its defences, and anything blocking the flow determine whether the river can take a level rise or not.

The capacity of the river is how much water it can take. This is very much tied into the second thing, the river defences (or the sides of the river). If it's a wide river with high sides, then it will be able to carry more water than a narrower one, with muddy banks. In emotional terms, this is about resilience and emotional strength. Basically, how much crap can you take before you break? Some people fall at the first hurdle, while others seem to be able to withstand all sorts of crap in their life, and they're still smiling. The difference between them is emotional resilience and strength. How easy do you find it to defend yourself from stress? Are you able to find ways to manage your stress and keep it flowing out as quickly as it's coming in? If you can't, then it's going to build up. Exercise, meditation, and relaxation can play such an important role in managing stress, but if stress-reducing activities like these don't feature in your life, then the stress will build up until you break.

The other thing that can affect your river is whether there is anything blocking the flow. In river terms, we could be talking about a fallen tree or some buildup of river sludge. A fallen tree is usually a result of some kind of event like a storm, and, in emotional terms, we could be talking about an event in our lives that has left its mark and made it difficult for us to handle life. Our lives are full of events like this and they range from the twig-like events that we can brush off relatively easily and that don't have much impact (like a rude person in the supermarket), all the way to the felling of the big trees that are holding up the river banks.

These might be life traumas or events such as divorce or the loss of a loved one. Now if there's just the one tree or just the odd twig falling into the river, we don't have too much to worry about. But if you get a few of these life events happening to you over a short period, they can quickly start blocking your emotional flow.

Keep in mind that emotions are dynamic. The word *emotion* comes from energy in motion, and this is a key thing to understand about emotions. We experience emotions as a form of communication that's being expressed to us through our mind and body. Once the message is communicated, there is no need for it to continue to be transmitted. Nobody likes hearing the same thing repeatedly; after a while, it wears you down.

To get a sense of what a healthy emotional response looks like, just watch toddlers. They're like little, fresh and clear rivers without any crap blocking their flow. One minute, their giddy with excitement as the ice-cream has been brought out of the freezer. They're given a cone, which they lick with gusto, and the ball of ice-cream falls on the floor. They cry and sob their eyes out. The ball of ice-cream is replaced and it's all smiles again. All in the space of three minutes! Their emotions are flowing. You'll rarely find a toddler in a sulk for longer than an hour. They simply don't hold onto their emotions in the way that adults can. They can let things go, which is something that more of us need to get back to.

Now back to the river, and let's talk about the sludge. The sludge is the undercurrent of negative emotion that forms part of our emotional experience. All rivers have sludge, so it being there isn't a problem. The problem arises when it builds up and starts making the water murky, eventually getting so bad it starts clogging things up and suffocating the wildlife.

In emotional terms, it's the same. It's totally okay to experience negative emotions like fear, anxiety, shame, or guilt. The problem comes when those emotions form the mainstay of your emotional experience. If emotions like joy, gratitude, delight, and excitement aren't there in sufficient quantities, then you're heading for a sludgy mess.

Every now and then, a life event happens that creates a load of sludge, and that's okay. In time, it will wash away. But with too many of these, combined with some big trees blocking the river and your river defences failing, it's easy to see how you're going to hit some emotional problems.

The other important aspect of our water cycle is the sky, more specifically, the clouds! In our metaphor, the clouds represent our values and our beliefs. Earlier, I talked about some lovely white fluffy clouds. Well, these clouds are out when our emotional skyscape is populated by beliefs that support and empower us, and values that are aligned.

When a belief is supporting and empowering us, it can carry us far. Beliefs like "I am awesome," "I always do brilliantly," and "people love to spend time with me" make great white fluffy clouds. On the other hand, if your head is full of beliefs like "I'm never going to get a job," "No-one's going to buy what I'm selling," "No-one wants to spend time with me," and "I'm useless," then you're more likely to be getting the dark heavy clouds full of heavy rain. Mmmm... I wonder how that constant heavy rain is going to affect our river... what do you think?

Earlier, I mentioned that the clouds represent our values. Ideally, our values need to be aligned, and in cloud terms, this means that they're moving in the same direction. Your values are your unwritten rules of behaviour. So, when your values are aligned with each other, they give you clear direction and focus. Compare this to values that are in conflict, where one value is pulling you in a different direction to another. This is conflict. You're torn. Until you can find a way for your values to be aligned, you'll experience stress. The conflict that arises from your values pointing and pulling in various directions will send you spinning in circles. In cloud terms, we're starting to see tornadoes and cyclones, which are going to play havoc with our river and the trees on its banks.

Over the next chapters, I'm going to explore values, beliefs and emotions in more detail so that you can start eliminating the sources of your head trash.

NINE

Your Values

_____

Our values are those things that are really important to us. In fact, they're so important that they act like the unwritten rules that we live by. They come from our culture, our upbringing, and our life experiences; they shape who we are and determine the people we choose to surround ourselves with. Our core values will rarely change in life, but our broader collection of values will shift as we move through life and experience the events that define our lives. If we lose a loved one or experience a life-threatening illness, we may reassess the relative position that achievement or success has held in our value hierarchy and perhaps shift our focus toward health or family. Just as the onset of parenthood often brings about a shift in values as parents come to terms with their new family experience.

Incredibly, many people aren't aware of their values, so they don't always realise how a big a role their values play in their day-to-day life experience. When I worked as a personal brand coach, part of the work I undertook with my clients was to help them to reconnect to their values. If we're to build a strong and authentic personal brand, then living and expressing your values consistently is important. This is very hard to do when you don't know what they are.

When you come across people who aren't authentic or whom you don't trust for some reason, part of this may well be due to a mismatch in the expression of their values. In other words, a gap exists between what they *think* are their values and what their behaviour *tells* us about their values. Someone can believe (and say) that family is very important, but act in a way that says the opposite. When people project this mismatch, it can affect their ability to build trust and rapport, and it will ultimately affect their level of influence. So, in business and leadership, being inauthentic can have disastrous consequences.

Emotionally speaking, our values are very important. Unfortunately, they're also at the root of most of our personal angst. This is because we love them so much; they're so important to us that we have invested a lot emotionally in them. This makes us vulnerable emotionally because it means that we're much more open to being offended or affected by the behavior of other people, especially those who don't share our values and who dare to tread all over them.

Swearing is a great example here. For some people, swearing is a big no-no and they consider it a sign of someone who lacks respect, while there are others who swear all the time. The cursors probably don't link it to respect; for them it might well be a way of expressing themselves.

Of course, there are those who swear in an offensive manner. It's easy to spot this kind of behaviour because it would be perceived as offensive even if they didn't swear. In other words, it's not the swearing that's making their behaviour offensive, it's the intent behind what they're saying and the tone in which they're saying it.

When people who don't like swearing come into contact with those who litter their day-to-day language with swearing, you can often see the reaction take over. The very words are triggering them and an emotional reaction is under way. They may either react and say something, or stifle it. The thing is, stifling it will be bringing some kind of stress to their emotional system. Holding back an emotional reaction requires effort, and if you're really offended, then this will be pretty tricky.

When someone behaves in a way that's in conflict with our value it can really hit us hard and we often take their behaviour personally. The problem with this is that often, their behaviour might not have even been directed at us, and we had no business in taking it personally. It was our values that sucked us in.

Let's take politeness. A lot of people value politeness; well, they do here in the UK, often to their detriment! So, hopefully, this is one you can relate to. This might not be a top value for you, but it could very well be guiding your day-to-day behavior, especially if one of your values is respect. Tell me, what happens when you come across someone who interrupts you when you're speaking? Then, they pretty much ignore what you've said and then speak *at* you rather than *with* you. How would that make you feel? If politeness or respect is a thing for you, then this might get your prickles up. This is because of all the emotional energy you've invested into your values; emotional stuff is being stirred up. Now, if this happens once or twice a week, then we haven't got too much of a problem on our hands. But if it's happening several times a day, then this could be amounting to a ton of internal stress. Over time, this will start to build up and wear you down.

If we clear out the emotional energy that's connected to our values, there is less emotion to be stirred up, which means that people can act in a way that's in conflict with them and it won't wind us up as much. Sure, you probably won't like it, but you're more likely to be able to shrug it off and less likely to get in a state about it. This can have a huge a difference on your day-to-day life experience; you'll feel less stressed for starters!

In clearing the emotional energy contained in our values, we can go a long way to reduce the day-to-day emotional stress and discomfort. Just imagine how many moments happen in any given day where you feel annoyed by other people, perhaps by something they've done or said. You might not even know these people. They might be people you've overheard nearby or on the TV or radio.

Every time this happens, your emotions get stirred up and you're adding emotional stress to your system. Think back to the metaphor about lakes that I shared earlier; your Stress Lake is being filled up daily by occurrences like this. How long are you going to let this happen? At what point is this excess emotional energy going to spill over into the Anxiety Lake? Maybe you're there already, or maybe you're already in Lake Depression territory. Wherever you are on this path, one way to start having an impact is to work on your values.

Now, I do need to make one thing super clear. Working on your values won't *change* your values; it simply takes the emotional intensity out of them. This enables you to:

- Be less susceptible to being triggered emotionally.
- Consider other alternative ways of thinking or behaving that offer more freedom, choice, and flexibility in your life
- Stand your ground much more calmly and clearly without being overwhelmed by emotion.

Ultimately, this gives you more emotional strength and resilience.

TEN

How Your Values Give You Head Trash

I 've already hinted at how your values can be a source of head trash, but I'd like to dive more into this because it can help you to figure out what might be going on for you. There are four ways that your values can take up head space.

Your values will add to your head trash when they are

- In conflict
- Out of balance
- Misguided
- Trodden on by others

Your values give you head trash when...

... they are in conflict

Our values guide us through life and we use them subconsciously to make decisions. Problems arise when we have values that are pulling us in different directions. The strongest value will tend to win the war, but occasionally a weaker value may win the battle and this can lead to some zig zagging in life as you feel the pull between different directions. This can make you feel stuck or torn, unable to move forward. It can also feed a terrible self-sabotage habit.

Let me tell you about Steve. Steve has a successful career in management and works for a large global company. He's considered a bit of a rising star and his boss has told him that he has the potential to make it to the board in a few years. This makes Steve very happy because he works hard and success is important to him. Also, he's a family man and would love to be able to provide for his family in this way. The thing is, Steve's job demands a lot from him, and he's not at home as much as he'd like to be. If it's not the late nights at the office, then it's the frequent trips away. Steve hates being away from his family so frequently, but he doesn't feel he has much choice. When he's away, he often finds himself drawn to the hotel bar to help distract him and he's put on some weight. This just feeds his guilt even more.

In this situation, Steve's family and achievement values are in conflict, causing him to feel guilt. The conflict is also contributing to him feeling like he's stuck and has no choice in the situation; he feels that if he is to succeed and provide for his family in the way he wants, he needs to continue with his current trajectory. But is that the only way? Maybe there are other options available to him that he simply can't see. The hotel bar isn't the only option in the evening, but when we feel stuck, we don't always make choices that are good for us.

... they're misguided

Sometimes our values don't come from our *actual* love for them, but from hating their opposites. Earlier, I talked about selfishness; well let's get back to selfishness because it's something we can all relate to. People who hate selfishness often find themselves loving generosity or putting others first. Is that you?

Let me ask you this: in the cold light of day, have you sat down and decided that you want to live your life by putting other people first? Unless your name is Mother Theresa, probably not. You're more likely doing this because you hate the thought of the opposite of putting other people first: selfishness. Selfishness has got a bad reputation so this isn't a huge surprise, but this means that you're being driven to generosity and putting others first, not choosing it mindfully. Big difference.

Instead of making a conscious choice about how you want to live your life, like Mother Theresa did, you're living your life at the generosity end of the spectrum because it's as far away as you can get from selfishness, which you hate. Perhaps a parent was deeply selfish and you're acting in reaction to your upbringing. You're not choosing it because it's right for you in your life.

When it comes to selfishness and generosity, the truth is that we need a bit of both in our lives; they come together as two sides of the same thing. You can't have one without the other. For someone to be putting other people first, there needs to be some selfish people playing the game and enjoying this person's generosity, and vice versa. It's like darkness and light; you can't have one without the other. They need each other to exist. All opposites work like this. The trick here is to restore balance. You want to reach a place where you're able to be selfish if it means standing up for what you believe in and guarding your boundaries. Selfishness is required to be able to give yourself some self-love and self-care. On the other hand, putting others first is helpful when you're a parent or a business leader. It's not just about you. If you make it about you all the time, life becomes very lonely.

Somewhere between these two polarities is a place of balance where you can dabble in selfishness when appropriate or dabble in generosity when appropriate. This leads me onto the next way that your values add to your head trash.

... they're out of balance

Our values are our values because we LOVE them and this means that we carry a lot of love energy for them. Unfortunately, this love we have for them gets out of hand and this means that most people find that they can't dabble; they're stuck at one end. And if they do dabble, it's not because they're choosing to; it's because they're doing it reactively, which tends to come loaded with emotional energy. I'm sure you all know someone like this; they make a song and dance about being generous. They buy rounds of drinks, hold the door open, let people through on the road, etc. But every now and then, they're outrageously selfish; they become what they hate the most. This happens to all of us; we become what we hate if our values are out of balance. And then we hate ourselves for it. Cue relentless mind chatter.

... other people tread on them

Our values are our values because we love them so. This means that when someone behaves in a way that's in conflict with them, we react. We get triggered. The thing is, once you get triggered, your default reactions kick in and you stop behaving in the way that you'd like to. For many, this means that you become what you hate so much.

Let's say you hate rudeness. This probably means that you value politeness and respect, so you expect other people to treat you with politeness and respect. What would happen if someone were to behave rudely toward you? Would you ignore it and carry on regardless? No! You'd react. At the mild end, you might mutter under your breath at how rude they are, whereas at the strong end, you'd become this awful, rude person saying it to their face - with swear words! You've become what you loathe so much.

In that moment, you didn't really have control over it; it was a reaction. You took their behaviour personally, and it unleashed your dark side. Cue constant replaying of conversations in our heads as we berate ourselves for how we behaved.

... you get stuck in your thinking

Right at the beginning of the book, I talked about rigid thinking and lack of flexibility, and our values play a huge role in this. When your values need work, not only are you more prone to reacting emotionally and creating situations that will mess with your inner peace, but it also leads to rigid thinking. The reason that we're unable to dabble in the dark side and do the thing we hate (probably the opposite of our value) is because we struggle to see the positive aspects of it. We can only see the negative aspects of it. There's good and bad in everything, the problem comes from being blinkered to one aspect. Let's go back to selfishness for one moment and explore this a bit more.

When we label something as bad, we're in denial about all that's good about it, which makes us less likely to dabble in it. Similarly, when we label something as good, we miss that there's also plenty of bad lurking, so we may not be prepared for it. Being selfish is often thought of as a bad trait yet, there is much good in it. There's a reason that the airlines want you to put your oxygen mask on before others; you can't look after others, if you're not looking after yourself.

By opening your mind to the positive and negative aspects in everything, you're open to the myriad of possible perspectives, perspectives that right now may not be visible to you. Once you have new perspectives, you're able to entertain new ways of thinking, which will lead to new thoughts. If you're trying to change yourself, a great way to do that is to change your thinking. You're where you are because of your thoughts. Thoughts lead to actions and behaviours. So if you want to change your life, start with your thoughts.

The other benefit of being able to see the positive and negative in everything is in tolerance. You're better able to see things from other people's perspectives, which means that if they behave in a way that conflicts with your values, you've got a better understanding of where they're coming from. You might not agree with it, but you understand it, and this can make a huge difference when it comes to personal relationships. You become more tolerant of other people's behaviour and there's less friction. That's not to say that you let people walk all over you. But, if you wanted to pick someone up on their behaviour, then you would be able to do that calmly and without emotion, rather than get into a heated argument.

If you want to work on clearing the head trash associated with your values, then it helps to know what your values are. Plenty of value elicitation exercises exist to help you with this, a quick search online will give a plenty to choose from. But at this stage, I don't want you to overthink it or get distracted by the elicitation part. You'll quickly figure it out once you start becoming more aware of the times in your life when you get emotionally triggered.

So for now we're going to keep things simple.

EXERCISE

Ask yourself these questions:

"What's most important about who I am?"
"What's important to me in life?"

1. Try to keep your answers as brief as possible, ideally to

one or a few words. You might start noticing themes or logical groupings to your answers. Once you've finished your initial brain dump, you might want to review and distill your list.

2. Now, prioritise your answers in order from 1 (highest) to whatever. This will help you to understand which are your core values.

3. Review this list and try to see if any of them are in conflict and pulling in different directions. If you think they are, put an asterisk by them, as these would be good ones to start with.

ELEVEN

Your Beliefs

B eliefs are the convictions that we generally hold to be true, usually without actual proof or evidence. Here's how a belief is defined in the Oxford Dictionary:

Belief [*noun*]

1. *An acceptance that something exists or is true, especially one without proof.* "*his belief in extraterrestrial life*"
2. *Trust, faith, or confidence in (someone or something)* "*a belief in democratic politics*"

They are often but not always connected to religion. Religious beliefs could include a belief that God created the earth in seven days, or that Jesus was the Son of God. Nonreligious beliefs could include: that all people are created equal, which would guide us to treat everyone regardless of sex, race, religion, age, education, status, etc. with equal respect. Conversely, someone might believe that not all people are created equal, which results in racist and sexist values and attitudes.

Everyone has an internalised system of beliefs and values that they've developed throughout their lives. These may stem from religion or may develop separately from religion. Our beliefs act as a lens through which we interact with the world, and we can see this in action very clearly when it comes to racist or sexist interactions. The beliefs of the individual affect how they treat others whom they believe aren't equal to them.

Our beliefs even include things that we believe to be facts. A long time ago, people believed the Earth was flat. Until proven otherwise, this was held as fact. Society holds many beliefs about what's possible, and these beliefs are being challenged all the time.

Recently, it was believed to be impossible for a human being to run a mile in under four minutes. Running and physiology experts said it couldn't be done. You could say it was fact. But Roger Bannister believed it was possible, and on May 6, 1954, he achieved what was collectively believed to be impossible. Forty-six days later, John Landy beat Bannister's time, and, since then, the four-minute barrier has been beaten by many athletes and the current world record was set by Hicham El Guerrouj at three minutes and forty-three second. This demonstrates very clearly that personal and collective beliefs affect your results and that just because something is presented as fact, doesn't mean that it is, and it doesn't mean that it can't be challenged.

TWELVE

How Your Beliefs Give You Head Trash

I 've already hinted that your beliefs can shape your thoughts and actions (and, therefore, the results you get in life), so let's take a closer look at this.

If you have the false belief that "I never succeed at anything," then you're probably not going to try to do anything bold or that will stretch you because your belief that "I'll just mess it up anyway" will stop you from taking action. Similarly, if you believe that "I can chat up anyone I like and can always get a date" then you're more likely to mingle at the speed-dating night, and that belief will shape how you choose to interact with those you speak to. Compare that to the person who believes that "No one finds me attractive" and "I'll never find a partner" and what success rate they'll enjoy by the end of the evening. Your beliefs determine the actions you take and the things you'll say.

Here's a great question to ask yourself that can highlight any beliefs you have that might be holding you back:

If you knew that you would succeed, what would you do?

This is a good question because it allows you to suspend your beliefs temporarily and explore what's possible. Once you've iden-tified the things you would do, then look out for the reasons you come up with for not doing them.

For example, your answer to the question might be "Oh, I'd start a business selling my designs" or "I'd move abroad and open my beach bar."

Then, if someone were to say to you "So, what's stopping you?" listen for your responses. These are usually beliefs that are holding you back. So things like:

"No-one will buy them."

"My work isn't good enough to be sold to people."

"I'm not a businessperson, I'd never be able to make that work."

"I'm not sure I could cope with moving to a different country; it's hard work."

When dealing with beliefs, any work we do from a head trash clearance perspective isn't about *changing* the belief but about *weakening* it and taking the emotional weight out of it.

It's quite probable that you like the beliefs you have, otherwise why believe them? It's also highly likely that if you like them, that you have invested emotionally in them; you carry a lotta love for them! This love energy is going to give your belief strength and if we are to weaken your belief then the first thing we need to do is to take the emotion out of it.

Once a belief isn't so strong, you're more able to challenge it and decide whether or not it's actually serving and supporting you. It's much easier to ditch a weak belief than a powerful belief.

When values and beliefs get mixed up and cause problems

It's all very well if I separate values and beliefs in my attempt to break things down and explain them to you, but the truth is that everything is mixed up. We might be experiencing conflict between values or between values and beliefs.

Let me tell you about Sue. Sue has her own business, loves

helping others, and considers herself quite spiritual. The thing is, her business isn't going brilliantly, and she struggles to build her revenue to a point that makes it sustainable for her. On closer inspection if you were to ask Sue more about her spirituality, you'd quickly discover that she feels that spiritual people aren't motivated by money, and that money isn't important to them. She's often heard saying things like, "Life is about connection and contribution, and being with the people you love, it's not about money and having expensive things." In fact, she believes that people who are motivated by money aren't spiritual. If you were to ask her about what drove her to start her business, she'd tell you it was about freedom and helping others. Freedom and contribution are important to her; they feature prominently in her values.

Sue has two kids and hates the thought of having a nine to five job. However, she's in business and, in business, money is pretty crucial. Sue's beliefs about how spiritual people behave appear to be conflict with the fact that she's in business, where money is a factor. Similarly, when we look at her values, we learn that her desire for freedom and contribution is what drove her to launch her business, whereas money isn't mentioned.

When we see how her beliefs and values come together, it's not that surprising that her business isn't going anywhere. In fact, her need for freedom has trapped her in a place of lack, so while she has been seeking freedom, she hasn't achieved it. This is a very common story among spiritual coaches and therapists. Until they can reconcile their conflicts and align their values and beliefs, they'll be stuck in this hopeless life situation.

EXERCISE

1. Ask yourself these questions:

If I knew that I would succeed, what would I do?

What would I do if I knew I couldn't fail?

Write down the things you would like to do.

2. Now ask yourself;

What's stopping me from doing this?

Write down your answers. Once you start doing this, you'll find that other limiting beliefs start making themselves known.

Write these down too.

3. Now review your beliefs with your values and see if you can identify any areas of conflict that might be causing challenges in your life.

4. If you find any that are in conflict, make a note of what they are. You can work on them later.

THIRTEEN

Your Emotions

I t is often said that *emotion is energy in motion.* Science is now able to show us how certain universal emotions trigger or reduce activity in certain parts of the body, and emotion expert Paul Ekman has been able to show that there are certain universal emotions that trigger the same facial expressions all over the world, no matter what language or culture. Our body forms part of our emotional experience; when we experience emotions, we feel them in our body. It's part of how they work.

We know we're emotional or experiencing emotions because of how we feel in our body. If you're stressed about something, then you'll probably notice a shortness of breath; tension in your arms, chest, or shoulders; and perhaps sweaty palms. This is on top of what might be going on in your head: a visual of things going badly or perhaps voices telling you how you won't be able to cope. Your emotional experience happens in your head and in your body. So, if we're to clear any excess emotional energy successfully and thoroughly, then we need to clear it from our mind and body too; otherwise, we've only done half the job.

Our emotions are there to help guide us through life and to help prepare us for important events in our lives. They also help to alert us to anything that may affect our welfare (i.e., avoid danger). The easiest way for our subconscious to communicate with us is through our body, our five senses (or is it six?). In order to ensure that we received the information quickly enough, this information flow completely bypasses the conscious mind. Let's say you're walking down the street and a car loses control and is heading for the pavement, your mind immediately senses the fear and instructs the body to get out of the way. In that moment you're not really aware of any conscious thinking process taking place, you just react instinctively. Once the danger has passed, you might still feel jumpy or fearful for a bit, but, soon enough, the emotion passes. This quick action is the energy in motion.

A healthy emotional response is one whereby the emotion rises and then passes. If an emotion lingers long after the trigger has disappeared, then we're in the realms of an unhealthy emotional response. If you want to see healthy emotional responses in action, just watch young children. One minute they're experiencing frustration, the next it's joy or happiness. Moments later, they're angry, and minutes later, they're laughing again. For them, emotions are flowing just as they should. False beliefs such as "boys don't cry" or "girls must be nice" clog up their system and start conditioning them so that by the time they're adults, they're like us, full of trapped emotions.

We experience hundreds if not thousands of scenarios a week that trigger emotional responses in us. Imagine what would happen if all the emotions that were triggered got trapped like that too. You'd have one big emotional congestion. Permanently tense shoulders or butterflies in your stomach. In fact, that's what many people have: bodies full of trapped emotions. You can see it in them and how it affects their posture, the muscles in their faces, and the way that they breathe. But that's just the beginning. A buildup of all this trapped emotion puts undue stress on the body and eventually leads to physical ailments and illness.

Positive emotions need to be cleared too

All emotions are like warning signals. When we have negative emotions, they're warning us that certain things in our lives aren't right; they're warning us not to go there. Extreme positive emotions tell us about the things we *do* want, but equally when something makes you feel good, it's usually triggers a warning you that if you lose this thing or person, you'll have a void and feel bad. It's equally important to work on the extreme positive emotions as it is to heal the negative emotions. When we over love something (needy of it) we'll hate having a void of it. The closer we can be to feeling good without the neediness the closer we can be to neutrality, which is a feel good state where energy just flows without the positive and negative emotional extremes.

Trapped or stuck emotions

This is when an emotion may have become stuck in our system, perhaps due to an emotionally intense experience. Because it's stuck, it's so readily available to us (it's near the surface), so we tend to experience it a lot. For example, if frustration is stuck, you'll add *frustration* to most of your life experiences: frustrated at missing the bus, at not finding a parking space, at having too many emails; everything is filtered through the lens of frustration.

Over time, our system can become clogged with trapped emotions that haven't been fully processed, and if our system is weighed down by emotion or dis-ease, then our body will start to experience disease. Many diseases have emotional imbalance at their roots.

Working on clearing emotions

When we work on an emotion directly, it doesn't mean that you won't experience it ever again, it simply means that if you currently have a backlog of trapped emotion, then you can release it, which should provide some short-term relief.

A good time to clear emotions is when you're in the thick of it, experiencing them. If you're overcome with emotion and would like to calm down, and return to a calmer state, then going through the clearance process will be a great way of doing that.

FOURTEEN

Emotional Triggers

E motional triggers are situations, events, thoughts, or behaviours that trigger an emotional reaction in you. Here are some examples

- People *lying* to you triggers your *anger.*
- *Being told what to do* triggers your *feeling out of control.*
- *Seeing a needle* triggers your *fear of injections.*

In his book, *Emotions Revealed,* Paul Ekman identifies nine emotional triggers;

1. Subconscious automatic triggers: You can think of these as your default settings. Some of these are our primal survival settings that have been in place since Adam and Eve. But a whole bunch of these resulted from your life experiences and the person you are.

2. Self-reflection (which triggers the automatic triggers): This is when you reflect on a situation that's unfolding as you try to make sense of it. At some point, the situation starts making sense and your default settings kick in.

3. Memory: You remember something that triggers emotion for you.

4. Imagination: You imagine something that triggers an emotion for you.

5. Talking about past experience: You recount an experience or memory from your past and this triggers an emotional response.

6. Empathy: This is what happens when we're sucked in by a good story or movie. We feel what they're feeling.

7. Others instructing us: When other people tell us how to feel. This can also be learned responses from others, as when a child learns fear from a parent by observing their behaviour.

8. Violation of social norms & personal values: When cultural and personal values are violated.

9. Voluntarily assuming the appearance: acting the emotion out, with our face and our bodies. It has been shown that if we demonstrate the physiology of the emotion then we'll soon start to feel it.

As you can see, the emotions we experience result from a whole range of different experiences. When we see them listed like this, it's not hard to see how day-to-day life can have such an effect on us. But it also helps us to identify areas where we may be able to make a difference in the level of emotion that gets triggered in our lives.

Let's take a quick look through this list to see what we can do, if anything.

Subconscious automatic triggers

Some of these are going to be pretty fixed. Those survival mechanisms that date back to the days we lived in caves aren't easily changeable. But some of our automatic triggers, especially those arising from our beliefs, will have some wiggle room. If we've experienced difficult or traumatic life experiences, then this will have an effect on our automatic triggers, but if we seek help in letting go of these traumatic experiences, then we can change the associated automatic triggers.

Self reflection

The more self-aware we become, the more we can have an impact here, especially if we combine that with regular emotional clearance work on those automatic triggers that we'd rather be without. Meditation and mindfulness can help here too as they can help you to create the space in between moments that enable you to make mindful choices from moment to moment.

Memory

Thankfully, we can change how we feel about past events by doing emotional clearance work. This is true whether the experience was traumatic or not. We can change the emotional association we have with something by clearing the excess emotional energy from it.

Imagination

A lot of fears fall into this category when people imagine a future event and fear it. They're not remembering but imagining. We have the power to choose what we focus our mind on, so this is completely within our scope of control.

Empathy

Would you want to switch this off? Probably not if we're talking about being able to get sucked into a great movie, but if your work involves working with sadness and tragedy every day, then you probably would want to take steps to protect yourself from emotional burnout or compassion fatigue.

Others instructing us

Let's say you've been wronged in some way. Maybe a relationship has gone south or your boss has been a total douchebag. You meet your friend for lunch and they get you all worked up about how you've been wronged and why you need to take action to sort it out. Over the course of your lunch, your friend has told you how you have a right to be angry, and in so doing, has made you angry. This happens a lot!

Violation of values

I talked about this a few chapters back, so I'm not going to repeat myself. Suffice to say, this is a huge opportunity to reduce the level of emotional energy being triggered by personal and cultural values.

Voluntarily assuming the appearance

This is totally up for grabs. Neuro-Linguistic Programming (NLP) uses this a lot. If you want to feel confident or happy then stop slouching, stand up straight, smile, and look up. If you do, then you'll soon start to feel better. Our physiology can influence our thoughts very powerfully, so this is a good one to bear in mind.

Working with your emotional triggers is a really powerful way of minimising the occurrence of some of the negative emotions in your life.

Just take a moment to think about all the times in your day when you are annoyed or irritated by others. Now consider all those the moments where people make you mad or downright angry. For most of us who spend time around others (hermits not included here!) this will amount to quite a few. And now imagine what your life would be like if you weren't bothered by any of this and just be able to shrug them off. This is peace!

By addressing the things that make you feel fearful, stressful or anxious, you're able to reduce the amount of fear, stress, and anxiety you experience. This, of course, applies to any emotion that you feel you are experiencing in excess.

FIFTEEN

How Your Emotions Give You Head Trash

Our emotions have a lot to answer for, at least when it comes to our head trash. Of course, our emotions are an essential component of our everyday lives, but they sometimes run amok and cause trouble.

Here are three ways that your emotions can give you head trash;

1. The Wrong Emotion is Triggered

Sometimes, the wrong emotion comes up. If you're not in actual danger, then you shouldn't be experiencing fear. If you are experiencing fear, then you're triggering the wrong emotion. This is more than likely because it's trapped and lurking near the surface, just waiting to be triggered.

A healthy emotional place means experiencing the correct emotion for the situation.

2. The Emotion is Explosive

Imagine that someone has taken your parking space *right in front of your nose!* Wouldn't that make you mad? Here we would be expect to notice some kind of response, perhaps a rise in tension in your arms and shoulders or maybe some gritting of the teeth. But if you feel the need to bash them over the head with a baseball bat, then it would be fair to say that you're experiencing an inappropriate level of emotion.

A healthy emotional place means experiencing the emotion in the appropriate amount or intensity.

3. The Emotion is Suppressed

Let's say something makes you so damn angry you could scream. But because you fear conflict (or maybe you don't trust yourself to be able to respond appropriately), instead of expressing your anger, you bottle it up and give them the silent treatment. Then, three days later, you explode on them because of a tiny totally unrelated thing. The problem with suppressing emotion like this is that it will come out eventually and, until it does, your body will be taking the strain. As with all excess waste, it's better out than in!

A healthy emotional place means expressing the emotion appropriately and acknowledging it.

EXERCISE

Great questions to ask yourself are:

- What situations make me [insert emotion]?
- What behaviour in others makes me [insert emotion]?

Answering these questions can uncover many of your emotional triggers for a wide variety of things, and if you take the time to work on each of these triggers, then you'll notice a huge shift in your emotional wellbeing.

SIXTEEN

When Head Trash Strikes

H ow do you know that you're stressed? When people learn that I clear head trash for my work, I'm often greeted with a knowing look and the confession: "I've got head trash!" People don't hesitate; they just KNOW!

So how do we *know* that we have head trash? What's going on that tells us that we have it? And by contrast, how would we, therefore, know that our head trash has now gone? To answer this, we need to zoom right into the second-by-second moments of our existence.

Given that we've agreed that head trash is stuff that takes us away from being our calm, happy, and contented selves, then it would be fair to say that we've been struck by head trash whenever we're NOT calm, happy, and contented.

So how do we know that we're NOT calm, happy, or contented? What's going on in that moment that tells us this? Think about yourself. Right now, how are you feeling? Perhaps you're feeling relaxed because you're reading. But now that I've asked you to think about your head trash, maybe some feelings are creeping in. If so, what are they? What's happening now that I'm suggesting that your head trash is creeping back in? Is it mainly a "mind" thing? Perhaps thoughts, memories, replays of conversations, or imaginings of future scenarios are starting to fill your mind. Or is it a "body" thing? Maybe you're noticing that heavy feeling in the pit of your stomach return, or the tension in your shoulders.

It's quite likely that you have both, a mind-body thing going on, as we all tend to have. When we're feeling relaxed and happy, we know because of how we're feeling in our mind and body, and the same goes for when we're feeling crap; our mind and body tell us.

I'm going to explore this a bit more closely by using stress as an example, because we can all relate to being stressed. So, how do you know you're stressed?

SEVENTEEN

How to Tell If You're Stressed by Something

Y ou might think that you're pretty clear on what stresses you out and you'd be right. You might be totally aware of what stresses you out, but, sometimes, you'll only figure it out with hindsight. Often, it's only once the stressful event has passed that we realise the toll it was having on us; we only notice it once it's gone. Well, that's not helpful to us, especially if we're trying to stop it from affecting us.

What if the thing never goes away, always rearing its ugly head? So rather than just leave this thing floating around in your subconscious, I want to help you to raise your own awareness about your life stressors. It can be useful to think about *energy* when we talk about stress (or any negative emotional state), particularly *excess emotional energy*.

Have you got a friend who hates nothing more than other people being late? Yes? Are you thinking of someone? Okay, now imagine this: You've arranged to meet your friend, let's call her Jane, for coffee, along with a couple of other friends. You arrive on time to find Jane already sitting comfortably in the cafe with her drink. You settle down and decide to wait for your other friends to turn up before ordering your drink.

Five minutes passes and Jane starts getting fidgety; she's checking her watch, looking around to see if the others are arriving. Another five minutes passes and the fidgeting intensifies. But now there are strong sighs too. You ask her if everything is all right, and she exclaims (in a slightly raised voice), "Well, Steve and Sarah are late!" and as she says it, her hands start gesticulating with particular emphasis on the word LATE. Another five minutes pass and she starts ranting about how she hates people being late, and, as she does, her arms are animatedly helping her to make her point. It's not pretty. Does that scene seem familiar to you?

Compare that to the time you were out with another friend of yours, Sam, who isn't bothered about other people being late. She would be quite happy to chat away with you while waiting for your other friends. She might check her watch occasionally, probably out of habit, but it wouldn't distract her from the chat she'd be having with you. If, after ten minutes, your other friends still haven't turned up, she might mention that she hopes they're okay and that nothing's happened to them. Essentially the lateness of your friends is a non-event for her. It doesn't even cause a ripple. What concerns her more is their well-being. She's *neutral* when it comes to *lateness*; she can take it or leave it.

What's the main difference between these two scenarios? (Other than the fact that you'd probably much prefer being stuck in that cafe with Sam than with Jane.) The difference is *energy*. Jane's discontent with lateness brings up a lot of negative energy in her that needs to come out. It starts seeping out in her fidgety gestures, and as long as the trigger remains, the energy needing to be expressed increases. So there are deep, loud sighs that accompany the now more pronounced checking-of-watch and looking-around-to-see-who's-arriving gestures. As time goes on and the trigger causing the negative energy is still in place, things need to be cranked up a level to allow this energy to be expressed. This excess energy now starts to pour into the voice. The raised voice is then accompanied by even more intense hand gesticulation.

Now, some people might have a slightly different style. Rather than let the negative emotional energy seep out in a gradual fashion, as Jane did, they might try to keep it all suppressed. But this isn't going to last long. At some point, it will need to come out, whether it's on that day or much later. And when it does, it could be quite an explosion. In the meantime, the stress the mind and body will experience as they try to stifle this negative energy will be very damaging. Negative energy is always better out than in. You wouldn't dream of stopping a fart from coming out! (Unless you're in a lift!) Just the very idea of a toxic fart (it's waste matter, after all) being reabsorbed by the body is enough to make you realise that it's better out than in. It can be useful to think of negative emotional energy in the same way. The longer it stays in your body, the more toxic its effect on your mind-body system.

Without this excess negative emotional energy that needs to be released, we wouldn't see these types of reactions. And ultimately, what I want to help you to do with this book is to *neutralise negative emotional energy*, energy that, if it were being retained in your mind and body, would be quite disruptive and damaging physically and emotionally.

In order for us to be able to purge this negative emotional energy, we first need to identify what's triggering its expression.

To help you to do that, here is a list of the kind of responses that I'm referring to:

- *Hand gesticulation*: waving of hands and finger-pointing to emphasise certain words or phrases
- *Changes in breathing*: loud, vocal sighs, sharp intake of breath (stress response), shallow breathing (another sign of stress)
- *Change in the voice*: raised voice, faster delivery of words and phrases, maybe even tripping over some words
- *Tension in the face and body*: frowning, clenched jaw, tight shoulders, clenched fists

- *Posture*: leaning forward, rigid.

As you look at this list, you'll notice that each of these requires *energy*. The waving of your hands, the raised voice, the increased heart rate are the result of energy being expelled from deep within you, and based on what we're seeing, we can presume that it's negative energy, because these are rarely the signs of a super happy person.

This negative energy resides within you and its very presence already affects you in ways you may not realise. It might be contributing to some physical symptoms or conditions that you're afflicted with. When you come across a situation or a person who acts as a trigger, they're merely bringing something that's normally hidden to the surface. They are not *creating* that in you, and they are not the *cause*; they are merely the *trigger*, triggering something within you that needs to be expressed, addressed, and healed. For that, you can choose to be grateful, because without these triggers, you wouldn't know what you needed to work on. They're bringing you a gift.

This is a great attitude to adopt when faced with annoying situations and people. Life is merely presenting you with yet another thing that you need to do the inner work on. The world is simply a reflection of yourself. Once you purge the negative emotional energy that's triggered as a result of a particular situation or interaction with someone, then it's unlikely that you'll be affected in the same way by that type of situation or behaviour again. So don't get mad, just add it to your head trash clearance to-do list and say, "Thank you."

EIGHTEEN

Typical Causes of Stress

S tress is a killer. Seriously. It's the silent killer that over time is responsible for so much misery. If left unchecked, it will build and build, and develop into all kinds of nasties. If I could help you to banish stress from your life, it would be a major win. But if I'm going to help you to do that, then I think we need to get crystal clear on where this stress comes from. It's going to be different for each of us, but there are some common themes that affect us all. So, let's look at those first.

Medical Condition or Illness

When you're affected by a medical condition or illness, it puts physical stress on the body. As our body is an interconnected system, when one thing is out of kilter, other parts of the system are affected, too. On top of that, your body is spending its energy trying to heal you, so there's additional demand on your body, which will create some stress. But there's an added dimension here: how you *feel* about what's happening to you. In addition to physical stress, you may also be experiencing *emotional stress*.

Let's say you've got a really bad migraine. How are you likely to feel about that? Possible responses might include:

Response #1

"Oh, this migraine is annoying...I'd better take a tablet for it."
Nature of response: Mainly internal thoughts.

Response #2

"Oh, no! Not a migraine again! It's so painful! I can't wait for this to end."
Nature of response: Mainly internal thoughts, but some verbal comments too.

Response #3

""I hate this bloody heartburn! It's so frustrating! I can't I hate this bloody migraine! It's so frustrating! I can't sleep! My head hurts! I wish it would stop! Grrrrr!"
Nature of response: Internal thoughts with a lot of verbal expression of thoughts. Frequent complaining to those around you that might include gesticulation with arms, or the raising of voice in frustration.

Which one do you think would be typical of you?

Be honest!

You'll notice that response 3 is a much more stressed response than response 1. Response 1 is from someone who appears to be taking the migraine in her stride. The person with response 2, while still fairly accepting of the condition, shows a slightly shorter fuse with it; however, that person still appears to be coping with it.

Contrast this with response 3, which shows somebody who is noticeably stressed by his condition. His stress might be because this is how he responds to most things, or it might be because he's been experiencing this for four months now and it's REALLY DOING HIS HEAD IN! Maybe he started at response one, but the continuation of the migraines is starting to wear him down. Whatever the reason for his response, if response 3 is now his modus operandi, then his body will also be experiencing the stress response, which will exacerbate the migraine (thus creating a never-ending loop).

So, in this situation, if you could respond differently emotionally to your physical symptoms, then you could influence how much stress your body will experience.

Fortunately, this is something you can do. At its simplest, you can just decide not to get annoyed by such things. I realise it sounds easier said than done, so, luckily, it's possible to address your emotional response and tone it down, if not neutralise it entirely. Continue reading to find out how, but, for now, I want you to be aware that HOW you respond to something is often more stressful than the thing you're experiencing.

Physical Exertion

The extent to which this affects you will depend on your general state of health and well-being. If you're fit and in good shape, then this won't be a huge source of stress for you. However, if you're not in the best of shape, any physical exertion will contribute quite a bit of physical stress for you.

Now, as above, there's the additional element to consider: the emotional stress. How you feel about the physical exertion will affect your stress response too. Are you *resisting* what's happening to you? You know, denying it? Or are you accepting it? If you go for a long walk and then get lost, the combination of being lost and getting exhausted has the potential to mess with your head. In fact, it might mess with your head so much that you can't think straight for long enough to be able to figure out a way for you to get home because you're stressing so much about the fact that you're lost. Contrast that to getting lost at the beginning of the walk, at which point you might find it funny, brush it off quite easily, or see it as part of the adventure.

Adverse Reactions to Medication

If you take some medicine and get a bad reaction, it's not hard to see how that might stress the hell out of you. Not only is your body dealing with something it finds toxic, but you're wrestling with the inside of your head about what bad luck it is and wondering who's to blame. Is the doctor at fault for prescribing it or you for not reading the six pages of small print that came in the box? Whomever it is, it will replay incessantly in your head as you make the slow road to recovery.

Environment

Just thinking about busy, overpopulated, and smelly cities and noisy, open-plan offices is enough to get you stressed, let alone if you've got to spend most of your waking life in them. The busyness and the toxicity is stressful on every level and we can all relate to the wonderful feeling of being in nature and how that de-stresses us.

The thing to note about a stressful environment is that it will vary depending on the person. Some people love to be in peaceful and quiet environments and need their environment to be like that for them to be able to focus and get creative. Whereas others might find the quietness too stifling and find that it leads to them seeking distractions. Some people find that simply being in a shop that has a football match commentary playing on a radio in the background while they're queuing is enough to get their stress juices going, while others might not even notice. Some people thrive in busy, noisy office environments, but for others, it's a total stress fest that requires an epic gym session at the end of the day just to shake it off.

I'd like to offer a glimmer of hope, though, if you suffer from being in a stressful environment; this can be sorted! And it's not about finding a way for the environment to be changed, but in changing your response to it. You simply need to figure out what it is about your environment that stresses you out and then work on it. #Boom

Emotional Stress

This is the one strand that underlies everything. All of the stressors I've mentioned above can be exacerbated by emotional stress. In fact, any life experience will be made worse by emotional stress. This is the stress that arises internally when we're emotionally triggered or when we feel discomfort. Discomfort isn't acknowledged or discussed enough. Discomfort is a super mild form of stress, and it's something that most of us experience daily. It's not strong enough to call stress, but it's enough of a negative feeling to trigger some kind of negative behaviour: lighting a cigarette, pouring a drink, eating some chocolate, or some other kind of comfort habit. Many of us turn to these to shift a feeling of discomfort or emotional dis-ease within ourselves. We want to distract ourselves from feeling it, so we indulge in something pleasurable. It could just as easily be shopping, running, or gambling. The key thing to understand here is the motivation behind the behaviour. If it's being done to *avoid* feeling something, then it's probably something that will eventually have a negative impact.

So what are those things that trigger stress or discomfort in you?

NINETEEN

What Are Your Stress Triggers?

I f you want to reduce the stress in your life, then your first step is to **identify** those things that are causing you stress.

As I mentioned earlier, stress is caused by fear. We live our lives surrounded by fear. The various media manufacture it every day, adding to the universal fears that we all experience on some level: fear of the unknown, fear of scarcity or poverty, fear of being alone or unloved, fear of missing out, fear of being rejected... I could go on all day here. Thankfully, these are all things we can start addressing.

The stress response in the body can be triggered by low-level worry and distant concerns, as well as things you might clearly recognise as stressors in your life. Clue: if you find yourself saying "God, this is really stressing me out!" obviously, that particular thing is on your Stress List. But I want to help you identify those things that contribute to that low-level hum of stress that's constantly there, so much so that you probably hardly notice it. Nonetheless, your body is being affected by it.

Now, the surprising thing here is that it's not as easy as it sounds. Why? Well, because many of the things that contribute to your stress are bubbling away under your radar. You've become so used to them, you probably don't realise how much they're adding to your overall feeling of stress.

A few years back an Icelandic volcano erupted and sent a cloud of ash over Europe, forcing the major airlines to ground their planes for safety reasons. I was staying with a friend of mine in west London at the time and remember it being this huge story with people being stranded around the globe, not being able to get home. I really liked the area she lived in because it was leafy and felt village-like (for London anyhow). You could almost forget you were part of the London metropolis and I always thought of it as being lovely and quiet. But it was only when the planes were grounded that it became truly quiet: for the first time I could hear the birds singing, which I had never noticed before. She lived under the flight path and when the planes were no longer grounded, I realised just how noisy it was. It was only then that I realised that the constant roar of the planes was drowning out the sounds of nature. And there was me thinking it was nice and quiet!

Well, that's what life stress is like too. You're being affected by lots of background noise in a low-level kind of way, but together they're all adding up to an overall feeling of stress. The problem with this is that because you're already in a stressed state (fairly mild probably), it doesn't take much to tip you over into a notice-able or visibly stressed state. But once you get rid of these everyday stress triggers, you'll look back and realise just how stressed you were.

Now, let's get one thing straight. When I say, "get rid of the stress triggers," what I'm NOT saying is turn your life upside down and get rid of all the stressy people and things in it. Getting rid of or changing things like your house, your job, your car, your kids, and/or your partner would be a pretty hardcore solution to getting rid of your stress triggers. What I AM saying is to change YOU, so that you stop REACTING to those triggers. This way, those things can still happen and those people can still behave that way, but now they just don't stress you out anymore. Changing *how we respond* to life changes our experience of life, so that's what I want to help you with.

I bet you can think of a negative situation that's happened to someone you know such as losing a job. Losing your job or being made redundant sucks, no matter how you look at it. Suddenly your regular source of income is threatened and you're going to have to find another job or source of income. Some people will find the news of being laid off super stressful, and they'll panic. A ton of worries and fears will pile up: *What if I can't get another job? My life is going to change; am I going to like the new version? How am I going to be able to cope?* etc.

But for others, once they get over the initial stressy shock of it, they get excited or inspired to make a bigger change in their life. It might even be a relief if they didn't like their job anyway. Or they might see it as a chance to try something new and meet new people. They might still worry about income, but they're responding differently, and this enables them to take on a different, more helpful perspective that's actually going to help them resolve the situation.

This is what I mean when I talk about changing *how you respond* to something. You can't insure yourself against rubbish things happening to you, but you can choose to not allow them to affect you in the same way. Making that choice isn't always easy, as your default response is often hardwired into you. I want to help you to change this hardwired response, and it's not as hard as you think. But first, you need to start by identifying the things that are contributing to your stress levels.

TWENTY

Make Stress Your Friend

A s much as I'd love to be able to banish stress from your life, the likelihood is that for the foreseeable future, stress will never be too far away. So instead of fighting and resisting it, how about making stress your friend instead?

I've already hinted that you can take steps to put an end to being stressed by routine events in your life, but that's not all you can do when it comes to stress; you can also make stress your friend!

Now, as you know, I'm a big advocate of recognising the good and bad in everything. So, while many think that stress is bad, stress also has positive aspects that are important to acknowledge. Stress helps us to make deadlines and motivates us to take action, but, as with most things in life, it's about balance; too much of it, and it becomes bad. So we don't really want to eliminate stress, we simply want to have it under control so that we can tap into its positive aspects.

We want to embrace it! We want to be in control of it, rather than it being in control of us.

This idea is very much inspired by a TED talk I saw called *Make Stress Your Friend* by Kelly McGonigal. Kelly is also the author of a book called the *Upside of Stress*. In her book, she highlights new research indicating that stress can, in fact, make us stronger, smarter, and happier if we learn how to embrace it. The key message in her TED talk that really jumped out for me was this:

How we feel about stress is MORE IMPORTANT than the stress itself

I put it in bold because it's important and worth emphasising. This new research says that people who *believe* that stress is bad for them will suffer the damaging effects of stress, whereas those that *believe* that stress is good for them won't. This is true even if both groups are living stressful lives. The key difference here is the *perception* of the stress and not that actual stress.

So it's a question of belief! All you need to do is to change what you believe about stress. If you believe that stress will kill you, it probably will. But if you believe that what doesn't kill you makes you stronger, you'll become more resilient.

The reason for this has to do with how our body responds to the stress and how that response changes depending on what mental filter we use. When we filter the stress through the stress-is-bad filter, the body's stress response is more damaging than when we process stress believing that it's actually good for us. The physiological difference in response is staggering and if you're interested in the nitty gritty, I recommend you at least check out her TED talk.

I know what you're thinking. "Great idea, Lex! But how on earth do we make stress our friend?"

Worry not, my friends; I've come up with the three things you need to do to make stress your friend.

1. Change your thinking about stress

If you feel that stress is bad, then this will be important for you to do. This but is super simple. Just write down 30 reasons why stress is a good thing.

This is a great exercise because it gets our logical rational mind thinking, but it also forces you to think differently and get out of your normal thought patterns.

2. Change your belief about stress

The important thing to do here is to purge your negative beliefs about stress. This will create the space for a positive belief to take hold and grow.

3. Clear your emotions around stress

This one is easy. Just use the head trash clearance method that I'm about to share with you. For now, all you need to do is to add *stress* to your clearance to-do list.

EXERCISE

Think about the things that stress you in life. Find somewhere to start making notes so that when the time comes later in the book, you're sufficiently prepped to be able to sort this out. Here are some questions to help you;

- What are the events in your life that trigger the need to express a load of negative energy?
- What do people say or do that triggers a response in you?
- What situations trigger a stress response for you?

TWENTY-ONE

The Head Trash Clearance Method

B efore I share the clearance method with you, I'd like to tell you a bit about one of techniques that it's based on, Reflective Repatterning.

Reflective Repatterning is a therapeutic technique from the field of Energy Psychology (EP) that was created by Chris Milbank, and which in turn was inspired by the Tapas Acupressure Technique (TAT). Milbank is known for his innovative approaches in the therapy world, and in addition to being trained to an advanced level in many mind and body therapies, he has also worked closely with many of the leading figures in modern therapy, most notably Roger Callahan, who created Thought Field Therapy (TFT). I was one of the first people to be trained in this therapy, and I was thrilled when Milbank invited me to join forces with him in training others. I worked alongside Milbank for a number of years as he further developed the technique, and assisted him on his training courses.

During that time, we trained many other therapists, counsellors, and coaches, and I remember being constantly amazed at the level of change we'd witness in our students, and hearing their stories of successes with their clients. At the time, Milbank was a brilliant mentor for me and he really challenged my thinking. He was always encouraging his students to get creative and make the technique their own, believing that we would all have something unique to bring to it, so when the technique became second nature to me, it was a natural next step for me to make some personal tweaks and add new elements.

When I was pregnant and fearful, I needed to make some changes to it to make it easier for me to use on myself. It was conceived as a therapy to be used with two people being present: the therapist and the client. But I wanted to use it as a DIY self-help tool so I needed to strip it back and simplify it big time. When I was in business, I was often tasked with streamlining processes and making them quicker or shorter, so this came easily to me. In doing so, I also spotted opportunities to make a few tweaks and additions of my own to improve it as a DIY tool. The result is the Head Trash Clearance Method. I still train Reflective Repatterning to coaches, therapists, and counsellors but that includes far more than what's shared in this book.

What's Reflective Repatterning?

Its name is a good place to start as it can help us to understand more about what it is and how we can use it. On one hand, *reflective* hints at the fact that it forces us to take a look at ourselves and *reflect* on who we are, how and what we think, and why we behave the way we do.

But the truth is, *reflective* refers to how the universal law of opposites (AKA the law of polarity) plays in our emotions, values, and beliefs. In fact, this universal law is so important that it forms part of the very DNA of Reflective Repatterning and informs its whole approach. This very aspect enables Reflective Repatterning to be combined with many other therapeutic techniques to turbo-power their effectiveness. Reflective Repatterning works brilliantly when paired with techniques such as Neuro-Linguistic Programming (NLP), Thought Field Therapy (TFT), Emotional Freedom Technique (EFT), and Havening. It can also be used in tandem with many body therapies.

Repatterning refers to its ability to re-pattern our thoughts and behaviours. Quite remarkably, Reflective Repatterning is able to quickly neutralise our negative thoughts, feelings, emotions, and limiting beliefs, thereby offering us more freedom, choice, and flexibility in how we think, feel, and behave. *Neutralise* might sound like a bit of a hardcore term, but it's not; it's just a great way of describing what's going on.

Let's take a quick look at what Google says about the word:

Neutralise: make (something) ineffective by applying an opposite force or effect.

You see? It's the law of opposites making another appearance. By applying an *equal but opposite* force, the thing in question is neutralised. So when we're talking about emotions, we're simply neutralising the negative emotions using opposing forces to give us new ways of thinking, feeling, and behaving.

TWENTY-TWO

How To Clear Your Head Trash

A re you ready? This is where the clearance action begins and I share with you the head trash clearance method. This is how you're going to calm the chatter and finally create some head space.

Step 1: Identify Your Head Trash

The first step in the head trash clearance method is to identify your head trash. If you've read this book in order and have been doing the exercises, then you should already have a nice head trash clearance to-do list building up. But I want to talk about this a bit more just so that you're super clear. I realise that it might sound bleeding obvious what this step is, but I've seen people get the wrong end of the stick here, so just bear with me.

Things to bear in mind when picking the head trash you'd like to work on:

Keep it simple

Make an attempt to express it in its simplest form, by which I mean use as few words as possible. If you've decided that you'd like to work on "I feel chaotic because the kids leave all their toys lying around all the time" then you need to whittle this down a notch. At its simplest, you could just shorten it to "messiness" or "chaotic" and work with that. Long phrases are more likely to get you in a tangle.

Don't edit!

Use your own language and don't change the words you want to use in your clearance to words you feel you *should* be using. It can be tempting to self-edit how your feelings are expressed. You do this because you might feel that you *need to use proper words* or that the words you just used *make you sound silly*. These are just other things that need to be cleared; what is it about *using improper words* that's wrong or inappropriate? Why is *sounding silly* a bad thing?

It can be useful to think of your language and words as the tagging system for your subconscious. If you start by ditching the words your subconscious uses to describe this thing you're feeling, then you will limit the success of your clearance work. It simply won't resonate with you in the same way and your subconscious won't think that you're communicating with it and won't respond or play ball.

Clearing fears?
Make friends with the thing you fear first

Is your head trash a fear?

Fears make great clearance items and my experience clearing my fear of needles and injections proved that to me. But when it comes to clearing fears, it's important to bear this in mind; we tend to fear things we don't like. People rarely fear pleasurable things like cake and chocolates, but they might very well fear painful things like injections. So let's use a fear of pain as an example. This is a huge fear for many pregnant women, so it's one I've helped clear in lots and lots of women.

If we liked pain, would we fear it? Probably not. So one option is to simply change our mindset from "hating" pain to "being okay" with it. We can do that by clearing the excess hate energy we have for it. Once we're okay with the idea of pain, we're less likely to fear it. The truth is, pain isn't all bad. Do marathon runners fear the pain they might feel in their legs around the seventeen-mile mark? Do they interpret that as bad and something to be avoided? Not at all. For them, the sensations they're experiencing are framed positively.

There's no reason why we can't do this too. The same can be said of injections. Some people fear injections because of the pain. If they weren't bothered about the pain aspect of the injection, would they still fear the injection? Probably not.

If a "fear of pain" is on your list, then you have two options in terms of identifying the head trash that needs to be cleared;

1. Clear "pain"
2. Clear "fear of pain"

In fact, I'd probably say do both. You probably won't need to do the second one, but I like being thorough, and for the sake of an extra fifteen minutes work, why not?

If you're given a metaphor, use the metaphor

Sometimes, when we ask ourselves what's going on for us, we often express how we're feeling by using a metaphor. For example, let's say you feel stuck. When you ask yourself how this makes you feel you might say, *"I just feel like I'm stuck in a swamp with cement boots on."* A client used this with me once. What an image! No wonder she felt stuck.

If your response is a metaphor then use it in your clearance. Work with whatever your subconscious is presenting to you.

We tend to work on one thing at a time, so, pick ONE thing you want to work on and you're ready for step 2.

Step 2: Tune Into It And Rate it

This step is about connecting to your head trash so that you get a sense of how it affects you in your mind and your body.

When we get triggered emotionally, we experience things that tell us we're having an emotional reaction. Perhaps we feel tight in the chest, sick in the pit of our stomach, tense along our shoulders, or our breath speeds up or stops! We might notice images or videos in our mind as we imagine the worst possible outcome or replay scenarios. Maybe we hear voices, our own voice or others, telling us what we should have done or judging what we DID do. There can be any number of things happening in our mind and/or our body that's letting us know that we're having an emotional reaction.

Compare this to a non-emotional reaction whereby you're simply being in a calm state and not really noticing anything that stands out other than being fine.

If we're to clear stuff, it's useful to start to become aware of how stuff affects us. The more we take a moment to notice and observe, the more we notice when we're actually being triggered. Since spending a lot of time clearing my own head trash, I can easily spot when I'm being triggered by something, which, in turn, leads me to ask myself what exactly it is that's just triggered me. So the clearance journey continues!

So, take some time to tune into how this is affecting you in your mind and body;

- Do you notice pressure or tension anywhere?
- How is your breathing?
- What do you notice in your mind?
- Are there any images or videos unfolding?
- Can you hear any sounds or voices in your head?

If you're tuning into an extreme fear, then I don't necessarily want you to complete relive it and freak yourself out. But you do need to emotionally connect to it. The more you're able to do this the better; so get as close to the true feeling as possible. If you have a recent experience that you can recall, then use that as a basis for how it affects you. Sometimes, we don't have an actual experience because sometimes we're scared of something that we haven't yet experienced; we're imagining it instead. *It's worth remembering that when you're fearful of something you haven't experienced, you're making it up! Why not make up something nice instead?*

When you've tuned into your head trash and you're connected to how it makes you feel in your mind and your body, I want you to consider how intense it all feels for you.

For example, let's say you have a fear of needles. Now, if you were to imagine a nurse standing in front of you holding a needle, you might notice some or all of the following:

- Your arm tensing in anticipation of the needle
- Shallow breathing as your fear kicks in
- Racing heartbeat
- Sweaty palms
- Sick feeling in your stomach
- Tightness in your chest

- Emotion rising in your throat

When you think about ALL the things that you're noticing, decide how intense all of them feel for you and give yourself a rating out of 10. If you mark yourself 10, then it's super intense and pretty hardcore for you, whereas 1 or 2 is a bit of a non-event, and not really anything that bothers you that much.

In therapeutic circles, this is known as the subject's unit of distress (SUD) and it is a useful measure of how much something is affecting you. It's useful to rate yourself before you start so that you get a sense of your starting point. That way, once you've done the clearance work, you can ask yourself again and see how far you've come.

The businessperson in me likes this because I like measuring things and knowing if they work. If I start at a 9 and twenty minutes later I'm at a 3, then I know I have had a pretty productive twenty minutes. Some people spend years in therapy and never shave that much of their SUD.

Make Notes & Track Your Progress

I find it worthwhile to make notes as I go through my head trash clearance. This is useful for a few reasons:

1. It forces you to stop and think. Putting thoughts into words has power.
2. Putting words onto paper has extra power.
3. It helps you to stay focussed on the task at hand. Clearing head trash can invite distraction; your mind might try to avoid doing this because you could be self-sabotaging on a deep level. Having a piece of paper in front of you helps you to stay on track.
4. You capture your starting point. Clearing head trash can be powerful and it can be all too easy to forget what you

were like. Seeing it written down in your own fair hand can be powerful as you later sit there, asking yourself how it was possible that you ever thought like that.

I've created a Clearance Sheet that I use to help me when I'm clearing head trash. It's a one-page PDF that I print a few copies off every time I sit down to do some clearance, I get out a sheet. If you'd like a copy, just visit here to sign up for the resources that accompany the book.

Once you've identified the nature of your head trash and given it a rating, you're ready to make a start with the clearance.

Step 3: Get Your Hands Into Position & Clear It!

Clearing your head trash using the Head Trash Clearance Method requires you to be doing three things *simultaneously*;

1. You need to be *thinking* of the head trash you want to work on
2. Your hands need to be in a certain position on your head (applying pressure to known acupressure points)
3. Your mind needs to be working through a psychological framework, in this case, the *head trash clearance mantras*.

Let me explain each of these to you so that you're super clear.

Think of your head trash

Your mind needs to be thinking of the thing you're working on. We're working with *thought energy*, and if your thoughts are elsewhere, then you might as well not bother. This is why it's important not to be doing anything else while you're clearing head trash. Driving, watching TV, or listening to music are all big no-nos!

When you're thinking of your head trash, it's best if you tune into it and focus on those things that you would have written down in the last step (tight chest, racing heart, shallow breathing, etc.).

Apply pressure onto acupressure points

The *Head Trash Clearance Method* uses the hand position that Tapas Fleming developed for her technique, the *Tapas Acupressure Technique* (TAT). I'll show you what the TAT hand position looks like in a bit. It can help to close the eyes while you do this to help you stay focussed on what you're doing.

You raise your hands into the TAT position each time you say a mantra to yourself. You might then want to take a pause, at which point, you can release your hands. Then go back into the TAT position when you move onto the next mantra.

Work through the *head trash clearance mantras* in your mind

You'll repeat each mantra to yourself for about two minutes. You can say these out loud or just in your mind; it's entirely up to you.

Practically speaking, this is how all this comes together: tune into your head trash, raise your hands into the TAT position, and start working through the mantras.

Lower your hands if you decide to take a pause in between the mantras.

Okay, so now I'm going to share the TAT hand position and the mantras with you.

The TAT Hand Position

Take one hand and put your thumb and your ring finger onto the bridge of your nose where your eyebrows meet, or where your glass would rest.

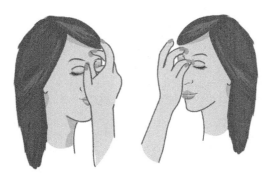

From the same hand, place your middle finger in the centre of your forehead. This spot often referred to as the location of your third eye. Here are the points you need to applying pressure to;

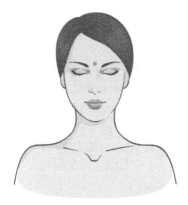

Place your other hand around the back of your head where

your skull meets your neck near the hairline so that your hand cups your lower head.

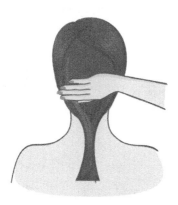

Switch your hands to find the one that you find the most comfortable but don't worry because you can switch hands during the clearance.

The Head Trash Clearance Mantras

There are ten head trash clearance mantras in all and each mantra has a blank space in which you insert your own personal head trash.

You should repeat each mantra to yourself for about two minutes, or repeat each mantra about twenty times. You can say them out loud or just in your mind - it's entirely up to you.

_____ *is a wonderful thing.*

_____ *is a terrible thing.*

I love _____ .

I hate _____.

I love other people _____ [being/doing/experiencing the head trash].

I hate and despise other people _____ [being/doing/experiencing the head trash].

I love making other people _____ [experience the head trash].

I hate making other people _____ [experience the head trash].

I love other people (or events and things) making me _____ [experience the head trash].

I hate other people (or events and things) making me _____ [experience the head trash].

Here is an example of the head trash clearance mantras using **frustration** as an example.

> *Frustration is a wonderful thing*
> *Frustration is a terrible thing*
> *I love frustration and being frustrated*
> *I hate frustration and being frustrated*
> *I love other people being frustrated*
> *I hate other people being frustrated*
> *I love making other people frustrated*
> *I hate making other people frustrated*
> *I love other people (or events and things) making me*
> *   frustrated*
> *I hate other people (events and things) making me*
> *   frustrated*

Until you become familiar with them, it's probably worth

writing these out in advance with your head trash inserted in because you might also need to tweak the sentence to ensure it makes sense, once your head trash has been inserted. That way you only have to read them out to yourself, rather than create them as you go.

Another great reason for doing this is that the thing you're working on might naturally suggest a dimension or mantra that's slightly different. Let me give you an example.

Quite a while ago, I decided to use the head trash clearance method to tackle my cat allergies. I had often heard that our body's allergic reaction is just our body's way of protecting us; it's just a little bit confused. When you have animal allergies, your body is eventually conditioned to respond in a certain way (the allergic response) and part of this conditioned response may well have an emotional component.

I felt that if I could eliminate the emotional aspect, then maybe I could reduce the allergic response, if not eliminate it altogether. I decided to work with "cats making me itchy and scratchy" as my head trash because when I thought hard about it, it was the thought of being itchy and scratchy that contributed to my strong aversion to cats. An aversion that they detected all too easily and that often led to them coming to sit on my lap!

When it came to the mantras for ME MAKING OTHERS experience the head trash, I stumbled. I should have said something along the lines of

I love making other people itchy and scratchy
I love other people making me itchy and scratchy

But that didn't fit; it didn't make sense to me in the context of this head trash. Other people had nothing to do with it. It was the damn cats! So I changed the mantras to:

I love cats making me itchy and scratchy.

I love making cats itchy and scratchy

And O.M.G! What a release that gave me!

The first of these released a huge well of emotion and I was sobbing uncontrollably, while the second made me laugh hysterically. By the end of that clearance, I felt like I'd been through the mill. I was spent. But I didn't know if it had worked and because cats don't really feature much in my life.

I eventually forgot all about it, until one day when I went to stay with my friend Steff. Steff had two cats and the last time I had stayed with her, I had been up most of the night taking my inhaler for my asthma. In the morning, I spotted loads of cat hair the bedding and only then realised that the spare bedroom where I was sleeping was, in fact, the cats' bedroom.

Normally for me, the thought of being in a cat environment would start worrying me well in advance of actually arriving into the cat-friendly house and especially given my previous experience. But on this occasion, it didn't even register as a blip on my cat radar. I don't even remember noticing the cats when I arrived. Whereas, normally, I would be primed on the lookout for a cat, just in case!

It was only the next morning when I was making my bed that I remembered about the cats; I saw some cat hair on my pillow. Then I remembered my last visit. And then it dawned on me: I had just spent the night sleeping in the cats' bed and I had no allergic reaction whatsoever. Not only did I not use my inhaler, but I slept really well. This was life-changing!

Step 4: Rate it. Review it.

Once you've done the clearance work and been through all of the mantras, you're ready to check in to see how you've done. So, just as we did in Step 2, now we're connecting back to the thing that we were just working on to see what we notice in our mind and body now. As before, you need to ask yourself questions like

- Do you notice pressure or tension anywhere?
- How is your breathing? Fast or slow?
- What do you notice in your mind? Videos? Images?
- Can you hear any sounds or voices in your head?

And again, when you consider what you're noticing and experiencing, ask yourself how intense it all feels out of 10. Remember 10 is super intense and 0 is nothing.

I'm hoping that you have noticed a drop in your SUD number. Be sure to rate yourself on EXACTLY the same thing as you were measuring yourself on before.

Step 5: Clear the opposite

It is now time to do the clearance work on the *opposite* of your head trash. Great questions to ask at this point are:

What would I be experiencing if I didn't have this in my life?
What's the opposite of the thing I've just worked on?

So, if you've just worked on *frustration*, then ask yourself what the opposite of feeling frustrated is for you? Feeling calm? Certain? Clear? Motivated? Similarly, if you've just worked on "being lied to" then perhaps now you need to work on "being told the truth."

There isn't a right answer to this question; it's very personal.

Here are some more examples to show you what I mean:

- Being ignored > being listened to, being given attention, being the focus of attention, being spoken to
- Rejection or being rejected > being accepted, being invited

- Fear of pain > fear of pleasure, acceptance of pain, loving pain, want or desire of pain
- Messy and chaotic (kids, other people, home environment etc.) > Being tidy, well organised, pristine, or museum like

Once you've identified the opposite of your head trash (step 1) you need to go back to step 2 and repeat the clearance process.

Quick Recap

Step 1 - Identify the head trash you want to clear
Step 2 - Tune into it and rate it
Step 3 - Clear it
Step 4 - Rate it and review it
Step 5 - Clear its opposite

Now it's quite likely that you have a ton of questions about what I've just shared with you. Things like

- How do I word my head trash for the mantras?
- What does a head trash clearance list look like?
- Why am I saying LOVE and HATE?
- This isn't hypnosis, is it? I hope I'm not telling my mind to think this!
- What happens when I do clearance work?
- How long does it take to work?
- What if my score doesn't go down? Does that mean I'm doing it wrong?

Well don't worry my friends! I've got you covered. I'll be addressing those in a bit. But for now, I just want to share with you HOW you do the clearance work so that you can refer back to this chapter and just have the info you want without all the explanations getting in the way.

I've created a handy two page PDF that you can save to your mobile device summarising the 5 steps. You can download this in the online book resources area which you can sign up for at www.clearmyheadtrash.com/book-resources-sign-up

TWENTY-THREE

Your Head Trash Clearance Plan

N ow that I've shared with you how to clear your head trash, it's time to come up with a clearance plan. How are you going to use what I've shared with you? You are going to use this aren't you? I know it can be super easy to read books like this and then never get round to doing anything with it, and I'd hate for that to happen.

I'm all too aware that the easiest way forward here is to do nothing, otherwise known as "I've read the book; that should do it!" approach. Then there's the reactive approach, which is actually a lot like the do nothing approach, at least in the beginning. Then the shizzle hits the fan and you remember this book that you read and think, *Ooh! I'll try that and see if it works.* In my mind, the best way forward is the proactive one where you take the bull by the horns, then look him in the eye and toss him into a ditch. If proactive is your style, then I have just the thing for you.

One thing promised you at the start of this book was that if you did the work, you could calm the chatter. Well you can, but this isn't something you achieve overnight, and it definitely isn't something you can experience after doing it once. For you to notice a real change in how you feel, it takes consistent action over a long enough period of time. But that doesn't have to be for very long.

When I train professionals in the advanced aspects of this clearance method, I split the training in two parts and the second training weekend comes four weeks later. The reason I do that is because I want my students to spend the intervening month doing personal head trash clearance. Only then can they advance to learn the more advanced concepts. In my opinion, you shouldn't be helping other people walk along a path you haven't trodden yourself. I'm pretty strict too. When my students attend the second weekend they have to bring evidence of the clearances they've done during the month and share how they got on.

What I love about the first morning of the second training weekend is hearing everyone's success stories. Those who have done their homework all report experiencing massive shifts in their lives. And do you want to know the best bit? The homework isn't that much! So, I'm going to set you the SAME home work except I'm not going to call it homework because that just makes it sound like a drag. Let's call it a 30-day Clearance Challenge instead!

The reason why this challenge works is that, there's an end in sight. It's short enough to feel do-able but long enough for you to notice a difference. Just like with exercise. You'd be hard pressed to notice any significant weight loss in a week, unless you stopped eating (and that's hardly sustainable) - but over a month, sure! I can tell you're excited about this, so let's get cracking!

30-day Clearance Challenge

The premise for this is super simple. Over a period of 30 days you are going to undertake one piece of head trash clearance each day. Now, if you've been paying attention, you might be wondering what I consider to be "one piece of head trash clearance".... Does it include the opposite? Well, the answer to that is easy: it's up to you! You have two choices;

1. Identify 15 things for your head trash clearance to-do list. Once you've added the opposites in, you have 30.
2. Identify 30 things for your head trash clearance to-do list and ensure that you clear the opposite at the same time.

Obviously, if you choose the second one, you'll get more clearance work done, But going for option one is still epic clearance work. So, just pick what is the most achievable for you. Bear in mind that doing a clearance that includes the opposite could take around twenty to thirty minutes. If you decide to do a clearance over two days, then you're reducing that to about ten or fifteen minutes a day. Easy! And totally achievable!

Decide on the approach you are going to take

The first thing to do is decide on the approach you're going to take. There are a few different ways you can do this, and the one that's best for you will depend on where you're at and what you want to achieve.

Here are some options for you to choose from;

1. The Random Brain Dump

This is a really obvious way to proceed and, to be honest, it's not bad. Essentially, you spend some time brain dumping, and then you whittle it down into something resembling a list and then you crack on with your clearance. This is pretty much how I started. Depending on how much head trash you have, this can feel a little overwhelming and the last thing you want is to be so overwhelmed by your list that you decide not to bother. The thing is, doing this in the context of a 30-day challenge means you can avoid overwhelm aspect. Just pick the first 15 or 30 items on your list and get clearing.

2. The Life Sort Out

This approach involves focusing on the aspects of your life that need attention. Perhaps you feel that your work life's a mess, or that your relationships suck. Or that maybe you're sabotaging your health and fitness. This is a great way to address those parts of your life that need some TLC. If you're struggling with identifying those areas that need work, then try using the exercise below.

The *wheel of life* is a great coaching tool which can help you to focus on those aspects of your life that need the most work. Or, at least to identify those areas where doing the work can restore some balance and sanity.

Step 1: Start by drawing a circle and then dividing it into six or eight segments so that it looks like a wheel. Then allocate each segment to an aspect of your life.

You can pick things like

- Relationships
- Work or Career
- Financial Health
- Spirituality
- Health & Fitness
- Family & Friends
- Fun
- Home
- Personal Growth
- Contribution

- Romance & Love

A quick search online for images of *wheel of life* will show you countless examples that you can use for inspiration.

Step 2: Once you've identified those that feel right for you, I want you to assess each aspect of your life and rate it out of ten in terms of satisfaction.

Step 3: Now draw a line across the segment at the point that represents the number you've given. Once you've marked up all your segments, take a moment to imagine how this wheel would behave if it were moving; where does it create bumps in the road? The idea is that you don't necessarily need to start working on those aspects with the lowest score, but on those areas that are creating the bumps and jumps.

By focussing your attention on smoothening the journey through life first, then you'll notice some real change in your life. Of course, you might have one area with a desperately low score that you would like to address. That's fine too. Go ahead with what feels right for you.

Step 4: Pick FOUR aspects to focus on. The reason I say four is that you can address one each week. But feel free to make this suit your needs.

Step 5: Now ask yourself what head trash you have in that area that might be contributing to your low score. Perhaps you feel that your career is being held back by a lack of confidence, or maybe your relationships suck because you're always having arguments and getting offended. Maybe your health goals are eluding you because you just can't stop comfort eating.

Head trash will be playing a part in every aspect of your life, and by focussing in this way, you can avoid the overwhelm and start making a difference that can motivate you to keep going and move on to other areas of your life.

In taking this approach, your list will probably have a combination of emotional triggers, emotions, values, and beliefs on it. For some, this might feel confusing or overwhelming, but for others, it might be the perfect way to proceed. Only you can tell what's best for you.

3. The Big Bad Emotion Clear Out
Another plan is to tackle the runaway emotions in your life. I'm thinking things like stress, frustration, anxiety and fear, or indeed any other negative emotions that seem to be dominating for you. With this approach you simply take a look at those things that are responsible for the stress (or other emotion) in your life. As I've already mentioned, the idea here isn't to banish these emotional triggers from your life altogether but to change how you respond to them.

A good plan of attack here would be

Step 1: Identify all the situations that stress you out (or frustrate you, or whatever).

Step 2: Identify all the behaviours in others (and yourself) that stress you out

Step 3: Use these to compile your head trash clearance list.

Step 4: Now add Stress to your list, and of course the emotions you decided to work on.

Pick two or three emotions that you want to deal with and you should have enough clearance work to do the 30-day challenge.

4. The Methodical Method

The final option is to take the teacher's pet approach, otherwise known as the methodical method. This is for people who like to "do things properly" (whatever that is) and proceed in a sensible manner. That is NOT to say that this is the most sensible approach or that the other three approaches are nonsense; far from it. You've got to start somewhere and anywhere is fine. But if you've read this book thus far, then some of you will be drawn to following the structure of this book, which means tackling things in the following order;

- Emotional Triggers
- Emotions
- Values
- Beliefs

If you're anything like me, you might feel that this would be the obvious way to proceed - *because that's how the author has mapped it out!* I get it! To be honest, this approach has a lot of merit.

By starting with your emotional triggers, you're starting with the lighter head trash; the stuff that hovers at the edges and that's pretty easy to identify and deal with. In trashy terms, this is litter. By the time you reach your values and beliefs you're dealing with more substantial trash items such as that old car wreck in the garden.

There is no right one to pick, so don't get bogged down by this and worry that you're going to make the wrong decision. If this is a worry for you, then add "making the wrong decision" to your list and just crack on. Whichever approach you pick, the important thing to bear in mind here is 1 - you have enough items on your head trash clearance to-do list to be able to do one a day; so fifteen or thirty in total, and 2 - that you stick at it.

To help you stay the course for the 30-days, I've created a 30-day Challenge Plan, which you can find in your online area here www.clearmyheadtrash.com/book-resources-sign-up

If you want support from a community of people who are already doing it then come and join the Facebook group at www.clearmyheadtrash.com/facebook/

Remember, if you know someone who you think could do with reading this book and you want to lend them a copy then that's great! But you don't need to give away your copy. I've created some things to give them a good flavour of the book which they can get for FREE! Just send them to this page www.clearmyheadtrash.com/get-cracking/ so that they can get hold of the Get Cracking kit which includes;

1. first three chapters for free
2. 15 minute video if they don't want to read
3. three 20-minutes audios that they can listen to in the car

When it comes to head trash clearance matters, it's definitely a case of "the more the merrier". For a start you are spreading the love, and that's a good thing. But, what you might not realise, is that you doing so could be JUST what your friend needs right now. Imagine that! I can't tell you how many times friends have given me a book or pointed me in the right direction just when I needed it. It was almost like a prayer was answered. But that's not all.

When you invite someone else on the journey with you, you create an ally or a partner in crime. These fellow adventurers can really help you to stay the course. Accountability and support on journeys like this count for a lot and can make the difference between you succeeding and not. And that's a good enough reason in my book. Especially if it improves the chances of you finding that clarity, peace and confidence you're after.

So, who could you invite on this journey with you? Make a silent promise to yourself to invite three people to join you. One won't bother and one will flake out, but the other one will be be there for you! Do it!

TWENTY-FOUR

Where Does Head Trash Clearance Fit In?

T here are lots of ways that can help you to reduce the stress in your life and get to a calm, confident, and happy place, so I'm sure you're wondering where does this fit in with the other stuff you might already be doing or that you're considering. I'm referring to things like meditation, mindfulness or tapping techniques like Emotional Freedom Technique (EFT), or Thought Field Therapy (TFT).

Meditation

Something like meditation and mindfulness is a practise. It's a lot like exercise for the mind. It's something you do regularly, and, after a while, you start to experience the benefits. How long it takes for you to start seeing changes in your life will very much depend on how frequently you meditate, the type of meditation you adopt, and where your starting place is emotionally.

Before I started my head trash clearance journey, I was into meditation. I used to go to my local Buddhist centre for their weekly drop-in meditation sessions. I loved the vibe there and I was totally in love with the huge Buddha painting they had at the front of the room. I really enjoyed meditation, even though it was something I struggled with. My favourite meditation was the mindfulness of breathing meditation where you have to count on every in-breath and then on every out-breath. The idea is that you count to ten, and if you mind wanders in between numbers then you start back at one. Well I never managed to get past three or four; I was crap! This is how much of a mess my head was back then.

I then took a break from meditation as I couldn't get to the drop-in classes because of work, but a few years later, I was able to return. In the intervening years, I had started using the head trash clearance method and I never really thought that it would have any impact on my meditation, but how wrong I was. I was AMAZED at the difference in my mediation practise.

Now, I was going past twenty with no trouble at all. The still-ness in my head and my ability to simply BE had shifted in ways I had never imagined. My meditation practise went to a whole new level! I felt that I was finally tapping into the magic of meditation and was able to really feel the benefits.

Now, I'm sure that I would have got there eventually with meditation, but I firmly believe that my head trash clearance saved me a boatload of time.

So, if meditation or mindfulness is part of your mix of tools to keep your head space in tip-top condition, then I would definitely not be showing it the door. Meditation is fantastic, but I wouldn't turn to meditation if my sole aim were to tackle my head trash.

Meditation and mindfulness help you to find that space between the trigger and your response, and create enough of a gap to enable you to be mindful in your thoughts and behaviour. In my experience, this can be achieved much quicker using the head trash clearance method, so if that was what I was seeking, then I wouldn't choose it.

Today, I use meditation to access the stillness and tap into my intuition. I love the thoughts and inspiration that drop in when I'm in that quiet space, So, I wouldn't stop doing it; I'm just clearer about HOW I'm using it and WHAT I want or expect from it.

Tapping Techniques

Here I'm referring to popular techniques such as Thought Field Therapy (TFT) and Emotional Freedom Technique (EFT) where you tap on meridian points on the body. These are often used as intervention techniques in response to something you want to shift or change, very much like the head trash clearance method.

However, there's a big difference. Those who do tapping often find they need to tap the same thing more than once. I'm not sure about you, but I hate having to do something more than once if I don't need to. When I've trained therapists in the head trash clearance method, many of them end up no longer using the tapping techniques they've trained in because they often find that they get better results with this (and they're not repeating the work they've already done).

Tapping techniques are fantastic as part of your emotional first aid kit, but they might not always get the best results for the deeper clearance work. Of course, this depends on you skill level and what you like using.

Neuro-Linguistic Programming

Even though NLP can be used for clearing head trash, I believe that it's much better suited to other transformation work. It's brilliant for improving your influencing and communicating skills, and manipulation (the nicest kind). The thing with NLP is that it's pretty technical, which means you need a decent level of training to be any good at it. Unfortunately, this also means that it's easy to mess up or fail at if you don't follow the steps exactly or aren't expert enough. If you're an NLP master practitioner, I doubt that I'll be able to persuade you to stop using it — and I don't want to

— but if you're not, then I think that this method will give you a better run for your money, especially for head trash clearance.

There are countless other methods, tools, techniques, and therapies that can help you in life, so I don't want to get distracted, but I thought it might be helpful to see how, by mixing and matching the tools in our tool box, we can actually get better results by using tools in a way that tap into their strengths, rather than simply using them for everything.

When it comes to building emotional resilience, there are many approaches. Raising your self-awareness is a crucial first step, then it's about boosting the positive aspects of yourself and weakening or getting rid of the bad stuff that holds you back. Then, when you've found balance in these two aspects of yourself, it's about bolstering it, boosting your emotional resilience, improving your focus and motivation, and continuing to bat away the stuff that might derail you.

Just as with our body, if you're overweight, watching your diet and reducing the calories is a great place to start, but so is exercising. Doing both is even better! And when you've reached your ideal weight, then you're more interested in toning or building up your skill in running or yoga for example. Our needs change as we move along the path, so it's good to know what can help us at each stage.

TWENTY-FIVE

Your Clearance Practise

P ractically speaking, what does a head trash clearance practise look like?

Adding things to your head trash clearance to do list

I'm always adding things to my clearance to do list. As the days go by, things happen, people say stuff and I get triggered. An email lands in my inbox that affects me, someone says something on the phone the bothers me; it never ends, but it's a lot less than it used to be.

Whenever something happens in day-to-day life that triggers me or causes an emotional reaction, then I take a moment to try to figure out what it was. Then I add it to my list. I might not do the clearance work there and then, but, at least, it's noted down for when I do have the time. Typically, my Head Trash Clearance to-do list on my phone is two to three screens long.

Things that have been on my list include

- Fear of injections
- Being rejected, rejection

- Being in control
- Freedom, being free
- Feeling trapped, being trapped
- Responsibility, being responsible
- Being told what to do

How often should you clear head trash?

Once you have some items on your list, I would recommend aiming to do some clearance two to three times a week at first and see how you get on. After that, where you decide to prioritise this in your life is not for me to say; it depends on where you're at in your life. At some times in my life, it's a daily habit, and, at other times, I might clear anything for a few weeks. But generally, I clear head trash about once or twice times a week.

How long does it take?

To clear one thing usually takes me around ten to fifteen minutes. This might be much shorter. I've cleared some massive life changing things in less than three minutes. Like my fear of needles and injections (which I'll tell you more about in a bit), and my fear of pain which I cleared in the final moments of labour in between contractions. But I've also taken longer to clear stuff.

It usually takes longer if we need to get more specific about what we're working on, or if it starts revealing further layers to your head trash. For example, I once worked with a client on *receiving* as they struggled with receiving help and money when it was being offered with no expectation of anything in return. Once we had worked on receiving, they still felt they had an issue around the money aspect. So we did it again but this time we worked on *receiving money*. Once we worked on that, it evolved into *being paid for work* that they had done. Once this had been worked on, we uncovered that they had an issue with charging people for work.

In this situation, we needed to get specific and in doing so, we hit upon some of the underlying issues that needed attention. This happens a lot. Our mind is a complex web and there is no linear or predictable path. We simply need to follow the crumbs. If this happens to you, then it's fine to simply decide to stop for the day and continue when you have the time.

When is a good time to clear head trash?

This might not need saying, but if I had a lawyer sitting next to me, then I'm sure they'd encourage me to say this: *don't clear head trash while driving or while operating heavy machinery.*

I would recommend doing your clearance while at home in a private space. If you happen to unlock a vault of emotional pain, you don't want to be stuck at the back of the work canteen in your lunch hour, desperately looking for a box of tissues.

Make sure that you have some time to yourself and that you won't be disturbed. Turn off your phone. If you live with other people, make sure they understand that you'll need to be alone for a bit and not come knocking on your door. It's not a good idea to disturb a clearance session and leave it unfinished.

Doing a clearance session late in the day can work well because clearing head trash can be tiring. If you're clearing something that's pretty big for you, then you'll become tired as the body kicks into healing and repair mode. This is ideal for trying to get to sleep. I often do clearance late in the evening for this very reason; it helps me fall asleep more easily.

Positive Head Trash Clearance Habits

I mentioned earlier that I've created a *Head Trash Clearance Sheet* that I use to help me when I'm clearing head trash. It's a one-page

PDF, and I print out a handful so I can get out a new sheet every time I sit down to do some clearance. You can find a copy of this Clearance Sheet inside your online resources area which you can get access to here.

I would urge you to use this at first because it will help you to become more fluid with your clearance practise. In time, you'll simply know what things need jotting down, but, at first, it can help you to focus. On this sheet, I prompt you to make all sorts of notes, but there are two things that are really helpful, especially when you're trying to understand if this is really working for you;

- The date of the clearance
- How you felt BEFORE about the thing you chose to work on.

These two pieces of information are brilliantly useful. The date reminds you when you did it, obviously! But this is really useful to know when you start seeing your life change all around you.

Doing this kind of clearance work is strange because, sometimes, you don't realise you've changed. Often, when we're making the effort to change something about ourselves, we're putting actual effort in. And it's the effort bit that reminds us that we're trying to change. We tell ourselves that we've just got to do this a bit more and then we'll get there. This transitionary phase can sometimes feel quite challenging as we adopt new habits. But when you just change, from one minute to the next, the lack of effort can sometimes mean that you don't observe the change. I've seen this so much with my clients.

Stuart was a high-flying exec who was in a job that was stifling for him. His boss was a fearful micro-manager who made his life hell. He desperately wanted his boss's job. He knew he could do it but thought that the only way he could achieve that level of promotion was to leave his current organisation. As a first step, we talked about him asking for a pay raise, as he felt this would be useful for job hunting, but he didn't feel very confident in approaching his boss with the "give me more money" conversation. We decided that he needed to boost his confidence so that he could have this pay-raise conversation, so that's what we worked on in our head trash clearance session.

When I had my follow-up session with him a couple of weeks later, I asked him how he felt after our session. He told me that he didn't really feel any different, so I asked him about his work situation. In the time since our session, he had spoken to his boss about his micro-managing ways AND asked for the pay raise AND HE GOT IT! But no, he felt no different! Thankfully, I had written down how he had been feeling WITH THE DATE and showed him. He was astounded with the difference and couldn't quite understand why he hadn't noticed it.

The thing is, once the shift has been made deep within, it's done, and no more effort is required. You start operating with the new thoughts and perspectives as if you had them all along. This is why you need to write this stuff down!

Some of my clients have now bought themselves dedicated head trash clearance journals where they keep all this stuff written down. One lady I'm working with is brilliant at this. When we have our sessions and I ask her if she's ever worked on integrity, she says, "Oh yes! Hang on, let me find it..." She flicks through her pages then says, "Yes! I did it two weeks ago. I started at a 9 and finished at a 4; it was good!" She gets a gold sticker every time!

TWENTY-SIX

The Principles of Head Trash Clearance

N ow I'd like to tell you a bit more about the head trash clearance method because I believe it will help you to get better results with your clearance work.

When I first started sharing it over seven years ago, I quickly learned that I needed to give people more than just the technique. I know this because of the number of emails I was receiving! You don't actually *need* any more information to be able to do effective clearance work, but it can definitely help, especially if you have an enquiring mind and are wondering things like *Why am I doing that? What does saying that mean? Why am I doing that with my hands?* Well, you get the picture! Before long, all these questions in our heads get in the way and distract us from just getting on with the job at hand. So I'd like to pre-empt this by answering some questions so that you can put your enquiring mind to rest and just crack on.

In this chapter, I'm going to share with you some of the key underlying concepts that are worth being aware of when it comes to using the Head Trash Clearance Method. It's my hope that once you understand these key concepts that not only will your questions will be answered, but you'll also be able to up your clearance game.

The Law of Opposites

The *Law of Opposites* is sometimes also known as the *law of duality* and one of the universal laws that exists alongside the laws like the law of cause and effect, the law of gender, the law of attraction, and the law of vibration.

The *Law of Opposites* states that everything in the universe has its opposite; Right – Left; Front – Back; Hot – Cold; Up – Down. Not only does everything have an opposite but it's also equal. In physics, this is reflected in Newton's Third Law: For every force, there is an **equal** but **opposite** force.

The *law of opposites* is one of the cornerstones of this clearance method and runs through it like DNA. If you're going to really get your head around it and achieve great results, it's important that you understand more about this law, and specifically how it applies to our emotional life.

Thus, I'd like you to imagine a see-saw. Now imagine that at one end of the see-saw is a huge boulder. The kind that my favourite cartoon character Wile E Coyote would always try and aim at the Road Runner. If you wanted to balance this see-saw, you would have to apply a force at the other end of the see-saw that equalled the force being applied by the boulder. Otherwise, your see-saw ain't budging!

Now let's just say for a minute that you happen to come across a boulder of the exact same weight and were able to get it onto the see-saw. Your see-saw would now be in balance. Hoorah! But, I'm not sure how long this see-saw would last with all this weight bearing down on it. If you really wanted the see-saw to be in balance AND survive, you'd be better off removing BOTH the boulders.

It's worth mentioning at this point that the universe is always seeking to be in balance, so if you hadn't found a boulder to put on the see-saw, the universe would have come up with an alternative solution to put this metaphorical see-saw in balance. This is why we have things like lightning and static electricity; this is the universe restoring balance. It doesn't always do this straight away, but it's always striving and moving towards it. Once enough force is applied, it springs into balance. Just as we feel the atmosphere changing when a storm is building. Suddenly, it all culminates in a thunderclap and lightning as the charges balance themselves out.

So, let's get back to our see-saw, but this time, let's replace boulders with emotions. Stick with me here!

I'm thinking you're an *honest* person. Am I right? Great. Well, in that case, let's imagine that at one end of your see-saw you've got a boulder that represents honesty. Now, as you're a big fan of honesty, it's a pretty big boulder. It needs to be to hold all the *love* energy you have for it. Honesty is super-important to you and you put a lot of energy into ensuring that you're as honest as you can be at all times. In fact, you also spend a ton of your energy, making sure that other people are honest too, and when they're not, it really annoys you. And why is this? Because you *hate* dishonestly. You hate it with a vengeance! It would be impossible for you to feel any other way about dishonesty. Dishonesty isn't really a *meh* thing for you... you hate it!

The reason that you hate dishonesty as much as you love honesty is because the universe is seeking balance and they are opposites for you. In order for you to love honesty so much, there has to be something at the opposite end that you hate with just as much gusto. It's probably dishonesty, but it could just as easily be something like corruption, fraudulence, or immorality.

So you see, when we're looking to lighten our emotional load, the place to start is to remove the emotional energy that exists around something. So, if you want to be less triggered by lying, dishonest cheats, then a great place to start would be by clearing the *hate* energy you have for dishonesty. The thing is, if you want this clearance work to last, you also have to clear the *love* energy you have for its opposite, which might well be *honesty*. Otherwise, over time, the universe will seek to balance things out and will eventually re-fill your hate energy tank. For lasting emotional relief, you need to address BOTH ends of your emotional see-saw.

Earlier, I said that the law of opposites runs through this method like DNA, and this is because it shows up everywhere. In fact, the law of opposites shows in up two important ways;

1. Within the head trash clearance mantras
2. In our need to also work on the opposite of the thing we need to work on

1. In the head trash clearance mantras
When I shared the *head trash clearance mantras* with you, you may have noticed that our ten mantras are essentially five, the only difference being that one is a *love* mantra and one is a *hate* mantra. The reason we're using two versions of this mantra is that we clearing the emotional energy from the emotional polar opposites of each one.

2. Our need to also work on the opposite
Step 5 of the Head Trash Clearance Method, is "do the opposite." Well, this is why you need to work on the opposite. As we learned above, if you don't work on the opposite of the thing you want to clear, you run the risk of it coming back over time.

So if you're working on your fear of something, let's say a *fear of pain*, then you'll also need to work on things like:

- *Love* of pain
- Fear of *pleasure*

If you're stuck on what's the opposite, Google it! It can be hard to figure out what the opposite of something is, so I find using a thesaurus helps me to hone in and find what it is for me. The thing to bear in mind about opposites is that they're unique to each of us, and what might the opposite of something for one person might not be for another. Just think of *stress* for example. When I've run workshops and asked for the opposite of *stress*, I've received all sorts from my workshop attendees: calm, joy, happiness, clarity, contentment, peace, etc. This is personal so just go with whatever resonates most with you.

Once you've successfully worked on both ends of something, then an interesting phenomenon happens; you achieve neutrality.

Neutrality

When I first learnt about neutrality, I thought it meant feeling neutral about something. It's easy to see why, but that's not quite it. In fact, neutrality is the opposite of polarity. And while that might not be immediately helpful, let me share with you some definitions of polarity to help you.

Polarity

1. *the state of having or expressing two directly opposite tendencies or opinions, etc.*
2. *the presence or manifestation of two opposite or contrasting principles or tendencies.*
3. *the positive or negative character of a word or other item in a language.*

In everyday life, we come across polarity in batteries and other such electrical items, and we might hear people talk of a negative or positive charge. To be honest, this is close to what's going on in your body; your body has electrical current running through it and your state of health and wellbeing is revealed by observing whether your body is in positive or negative electrical charge. Feel free to measure your personal electrical current with a voltmeter to see what I mean.

If you're in negative, one way to switch polarity is to state affirmations and focus your mind on positive emotions and aspects of your life. This can help you to switch to a positive charge.

If we think about polarity in terms of emotions, then when we think about what are polar opposites, the obvious emotions that come to mind are the most powerful ones: love and hate. So, it follows that we love some things and hate others, and our view is usually pretty fixed. If we love chocolate today, it's unlikely that tomorrow we'll hate it. So if we are to think about what the opposite of that might be, it isn't feeling nothing or neutral about something, but instead being able to love, like, or hate it. As I've mentioned chocolate, let's stick with that as an example.

Let's say you LOVE chocolate! And when I say LOVE, I mean you're pretty much addicted. I mean you REALLY love it. In fact, a day doesn't go by when you don't eat any. If you see a piece of chocolate, then you'll take a bite. If you have chocolate in the house, then it won't last long because you'll end up eating it. If you're offered some, you'll say yes; you'll find it pretty hard to resist because you love it so much. This might actually sound familiar to you! The thing about these chocolate lovers is that this is where they spend their days - in the chocolate loving zone, wondering when they'll be able to get their next chocolate fix. It's highly unlikely that chocolate lovers would ever wander into the chocolate hating zone.

Of course, there might well be people who HATE chocolate. I'm sure there must be! At least, let's assume there are for the purposes of my illustration. These chocolate haters will go out of their way to AVOID chocolate. They can't even bear the crinkling of chocolate wrappers, let alone the smell! Now, as with our chocolate lovers, it's very unlikely that these guys will ever switch to become chocolate lovers. They too will spend their days in the chocolate hating zone, wondering what they could possibly eat to go with their coffee.

So what's the opposite to this scenario? What's the opposite to the idea of people being stuck at the polar extremes of the chocolate spectrum? It can't be feeling neutral about chocolate because, if these people did exist they would just be sitting half way in between the lovers and the haters. So what is it?

Is your head starting to creak now? Spoiler alert coming!

It would be the *ability* to love chocolate, but not be totally addicted to it. There are days when you really enjoy it, then it might be days or weeks before you have some again. There might even be times when you're really not in the mood and you turn chocolate down! As crazy as this seems, this is someone who is experiencing neutrality around chocolate. They can love it or leave it. But it's certainly not a neutral feeling. Instead, it's an ability to eat chocolate mindfully. To be able to CHOOSE when to eat it and enjoy it, rather than being stuck at the I LOVE IT SO I GOTTA EAT IT end or the I HATE IT AND DON'T EVEN WANNA SEE IT end.

I hope that you've now got a much better idea of what neutrality is, but I need you to move your thinking on a bit further. Chocolate was a lovely sweetener, but I'm afraid it's served its purpose now, as I need to help you to get your head around the idea of neutrality when it comes to our emotions. So I'm going to ditch the chocolate and send you back over to the seesaw. When I explain neutrality in my training workshops, I find it always helps to ask people to imagine standing on a see saw. (Can you tell that I love see-saws?)

When you feel strongly about something, say you love it or you hate it, then you'll find it hard to experience the opposite. Let's say, you love respect, then it follows that you hate disrespect. As someone who loves respect, you'll find it very easy to be respectful to others, and will no doubt criticise or complain about those who display signs of disrespect. If you were on the respect-disrespect see saw, you would be standing firmly at the respect end, with all your love energy weighing you down. The more you love it, the heavier the weight. Now, imagine, for one moment, that you need to be disrespectful; perhaps someone is abusing you verbally and only a strong stern response will prevent them from upping their abuse to physical abuse. You need to be disrespectful to protect yourself.

On our see-saw, you would need to walk over to the disrespect end and express disrespect. But see-saws are slippery and you find it quite hard to walk up your side to the middle (otherwise known as experiencing resistance). You might even find that you're stuck. Stuck in a place of respect (the resistance was too much). You might think that sounds okay; after all, you LOVE respect and think that it's a good thing. But, as with all things, there are good aspects and bad aspects. Nothing is intrinsically GOOD or BAD; it's the value that we place on something that makes it good or bad. Something may be good in a given quantity, but too much of it can quickly make it bad (like chocolate).

When we clear the excess emotional energy around something, what we're actually doing is removing that energetic emotional weight to enable you to stand at the middle of the see saw. From this new position, you're now able to move to either end easily depending on what the situation you're in calls for. There's no resistance from your thoughts, feelings, emotions or beliefs; you have flexibility of thought and behaviour, and the freedom to choose how to respond (freedom, choice, and flexibility). This is neutrality; the ability to act mindfully in any given moment, with no predetermined default behaviour pattern kicking in without you thinking it or wanting it.

Here's another way to think about this. Imagine you have bunch of emotions that you carry with you everywhere, no matter what the circumstance. Let's say frustration was one of them.

Imagine frustration is like a heavy tool (big hammer) and you carry it around in your hand. Because it's in your hand, you use it everywhere, even if it's not required or appropriate. But you can't help it; it's in your hand. So, you're frustrated that you've just missed the bus, you're frustrated that you've got to the printer and it's out of paper, you're frustrated that the person in front of you has just ordered the last meal of the day... You get the picture. Everything for you is frustrating. Now, how about you get yourself a tool belt. Radical huh? Then, you can put the tool down and only pick it up when you need it. You still have it with you, but it's just not in your hand getting mixed up with everything you do. Having neutrality around frustration is like having it in the tool belt.

Freedom, Choice & Flexibility

In explaining neutrality, I talked quite a bit about freedom, choice, and flexibility. Well, I'd like to dwell on this for a brief moment because understanding freedom, choice, and flexibility when it comes to our head trash can be quite enlightening. Let me share with you examples that I hope explain things.

Imagine that you have a fear of flying. You would probably do everything you could to avoid taking a plane. The lengths you go to will depend on how fearful you are. Avoiding airports or taking planes isn't very freeing is it? You're not really in a position of choice because your options for travel or going on holiday are being reduced by your fear. The same would go for any fear; we deliberately take steps to avoid doing something [because it's too scary], so, in fact, we're being forced to follow a particular route of action.

The same goes for a negative emotion. Let's say you absolutely hate dishonesty in others. You wouldn't be free to be dishonest if the need came up because you hate it too much! You couldn't choose to be dishonest because, as far as you're concerned, your only option would be to be honest (not helpful if a robber in a black and white striped top is asking you for the combination code for the safe) and this is all because your thinking isn't flexible enough (and hence your behaviour) to allow for times of creative dishonesty in your life.

And what about any limiting thoughts or beliefs that you may have? Beliefs like "I can't possibly charge that" or "I'm useless at trying new things" are likely to stop you from fully considering all the options available to you. By reducing your options in your mind in this way, you're limiting your freedom, choice, and flexibility to respond to whatever situation ultimately presents itself.

The same could be said of a subconscious or default pattern of behaviour. When we respond angrily to little Jonnie for accidentally spilling the milk, were we really making a decision in that moment to be angry (a choice) or was it an automatic response that we couldn't help (reaction)? Are we able to be flexible in how we respond (i.e., not always showing anger), depending on what might be the most appropriate in that moment?

Often, our inability to act with freedom, choice, and flexibility causes us stress and angst. By neutralising the negative thought, feeling, or emotion, we restore our ability to act with freedom, choice, and flexibility, and this enables us to be mindful in our lives. Living mindfully helps us to live with less stress; it also means that we're better able to respond to what life brings us moment to moment.

Mindfully angry

Let's see how mindful behaviour looks like when it comes to anger. In this regard, I myself have witnessed a huge change in my own behaviour, which comes in very handy as a mum. Before I had worked on this, I would have been one of those people who cursed the house down at a huge spillage and then proceeded to be this horrible angry person for about an hour as it squirmed around in my system. Instead, today, I'm able to respond calmly and just get on with clearing it up and then move on to the next joyous moment around the corner that my kids will undoubtedly bring me. After all, they're just kids, and they didn't do it on purpose. If they did do it on purpose, then I choose to be angry, understandably. But the key thing is that I'm choosing to show that I'm angry and in control of it.

There are times when being angry is useful and worthwhile, particularly according to my own parenting style (which is not up for debate right this moment). Sometimes, it's useful for my children to see me angry and not happy about something, but usually it's because I've decided to be angry. Anger is a healthy emotion that needs to be expressed, and my kids need to learn how to express their anger; so, in those moments, I am leading by example.

What I'm not encouraging here is no anger, ever! Bottling up emotions is only going to go one way: BADLY! Instead, what I'm suggesting is a mindful use of anger. You choose when to be angry and the level of anger. It's controlled and measured; as opposed to this big emotional explosion that's full of curse words and abrupt movements (slamming doors, etc.). In fact, when anger is expressed calmly, it can often feel a little bit more scary, even as an adult.

When someone is angry and losing it (emotionally), it can be all too easy to dismiss them for having a moment. But when the anger is delivered in a calm way, the message behind it has more impact. The same goes with any emotion. If you can demonstrate an emotion without losing it emotionally, people listen. Just think of those topical news programmes where you often see heated debates (in the UK, we have shows like *Newsnight* and *Question Time* for this).

When someone is putting their view across and they're losing control of their emotions, we stop listening and start noticing the emotional reaction instead. If they're able to remain calm in those moments, our attention would stay focused on what they were saying.

The great thing about being able to do this is that you can let go of the emotion as soon as you no longer need it, rather than carrying it around for hours or days. So, if I'm with my kids and the eldest has just done something silly. Once I've shown her how angry I am about what she's done. I put anger down and go back to being "normal" (ha! whatever that is).

So, if that means being present with my youngest or chatting to my partner, I'm able to do that without anger. Now, don't get me wrong, I'm not perfect at this. I still have a shed-load of emotional triggers to work on, but having spent years clearing the things that trigger my negative emotions, I'm much better able to remain present and mindful most of the time, which, for me, is a huge improvement on the stress fest that used to be my life bubble.

The impact of using LOVE and HATE in the mantras

We've already talked about how love and hate are the most powerful emotions, so when we want to do some deep clearance work, we need to apply the law of opposites to the far reaches of your head trash, and this means applying it to each of the hidden dimensions.

Let me invite you to think of something emotional for a minute. No... that could get messy. How about a wet flannel instead. Yes. Think of a wet flannel. Now imagine picking it up. How would that feel?

Heavy? Weighed down? It would affect everything it came into contact with; everything would get wet! It would be a bit of bummer wouldn't it? And not in a good way. It would be a bit messy. In fact, when you think about it, this wet flannel is a bit like us when we're emotional; we feel heavy, weighed down, a bit teary, and we affect those around us.

But I digress... back to the flannel...

Now let's say that you wanted to make the flannel more manageable; less heavy, less messy and wet, and lighter. How would you go about doing that? What would you do if you wanted to make sure that as much of the water came out as possible?

Did you say you'd *twist* it in *opposite* directions? Yes! Wringing it in opposite directions would be the most effective way of removing the excess water; by wringing it to opposite extremes, we're able to remove the excess water and return it to a semi dry state.

Well, it's the same idea at play when we use the emotional opposites to remove excess emotional energy from each of the dimensions. We're going to the most extreme emotion in either direction; love and hate are the most powerful emotions after all.

Let's imagine for a minute that you really hate the thought of pain. Like, you really, really hate the thought of pain. In fact, you hate it so much that you've pretty much decided that injections are a big no-no for you, and you've opted out of certain medication as a result (this is a common health issue that has serious consequences and it's one that has medics scratching their heads for solutions). That's a lot of hate energy right there.

So if you're going to expel all that emotional energy, one of the things you're going to need to do is to LOVE pain. Like really love it! Love it as much as you can. Now admittedly, if you hate the thought of pain, this is going to feel a bit weird. Loving pain? Yes! But an important thing happens when you sit and focus your thought energy on loving pain; your resistance pops up. Or, depending on how much you hate pain, it might SCREAM, "No I don't! I don't love pain; I hate it! No! No!" And the more you sit with it, the more you wear your resistance down. Well actually, you're just wringing it out. And the longer you spend staying with the love/hate phrases, the more you wring out the emotional energy; just like the longer you wring a flannel, the drier it becomes.

Once you've gone through this process for each of the dimensions, you'll find that your hatred of pain isn't so powerful; it's lost its power and energy. So, while you're not exactly in a place that loves it, you're no longer in a place that hates it with such vengeance. This, my friend, is that lovely place called neutrality.

TWENTY-SEVEN

Frequently Asked Questions

I'd like to wrap things up by tackling some questions that I'm often asked that I might not had addressed already.

What happens when I clear head trash?

As I've already mentioned quite a bit, your body is heavily involved in your emotional life. We experience emotions through our body; that's how we know we're being emotional. We're feeling stuff!

I've also mentioned that emotions can easily become trapped. Well guess where they get trapped? In our body! This means that when we're having an emotional clear-out, we might notice stuff happening in our body as the emotional energy is being released.

You might notice things like...

- Tingling sensations in your body as you release the energy from where it's being stored
- A shift in body sensations as you go through the clearance mantras. For example, you might start by

noticing tingling around your tummy. This then shifts to create a feeling of heartburn, which then becomes a burp you feel rising, finishing with an actual burp

- Big sighs or yawns as you clear the emotional energy
- Cleansing tears coming out of your eyes as the emotional stress is released. This isn't the same as crying; they're more likely to be cleansing tears. That's not to say you won't cry or sob, though, as that's possible too. This is pure emotion that you're releasing, so don't be scared by it.

Whether you experience any of this or not doesn't matter. Anything is fine. We're all different.

But I know the question you're dying to ask me is actually this:

How long does it take to notice a difference?

It depends! In terms of the thing that you're working on, the change can happen instantly. Whether you *notice* the change instantly is something else. Depending on what you're working on, it might be that you need to be in a trigger situation before you know whether you've experienced a shift. For some people, it might take days for them to notice. Also, because the change happens deep within, you soon forget that this thing actually bothered you, so you forget to check in with yourself. Remember my client Stuart who didn't think that we had affected his confidence?

Let me share a story that I hope will illustrate how quick change can happen. You might remember me mentioning that I used to have a fear of needles and injections. Well, this fear was off the scale.

Ever since I can remember, the sight of needles would freak me out. As a child, I remember regularly fainting at the doctor's when I had to have a blood test. As an adult, I would be overcome with panic and anxiety in the lead-up to an injection, even over the days leading up to it! I once needed to have a medical examination as part of my work, which included an injection first thing one morning. If I told you that I struggled, it would be an understatement. When I eventually got back to work later that morning, I couldn't even walk across the car park, and by lunchtime, one of my colleagues had to drive me home. Ridiculous!

This was a situation that I was desperate to sort out, and I got my opportunity when I trained in Neuro-Linguistic Programming (NLP) with Richard Bandler and Paul McKenna. One day, our training was on phobias and we could choose to work on any sort: needles, small spaces, spiders, snakes, or public speaking. At the beginning of the day, Paul spent some time showing us what we'd be doing using needles as his demonstration.

We were in a room of about a hundred and fifty people and I was six rows back. As I sat there, watching him hold the needle on stage, I could already feel my panic rising; my palms were getting really sweaty and I could feel that I was losing control of my emotions. I thought I might cry at any moment. He wanted a person to do his demo on. Half of me wanted so badly to be rid of this, but I couldn't bring myself to raise my hand; I didn't want to get any nearer to the needle in his hand. The other half of me nearly ran out crying. Crazy, right? I mean REALLY crazy! What kind of a response is that?

I went to the needle phobia group and we spent an hour or so working on our phobia. I did really well; by the end of the hour, I was able to hold a needle against my arm and not lose the plot. This was progress! But alas, it was short-lived. The time soon came to have another injection. I remember thinking, "Hey, this is cool. I'm not scared." But despite this, my arm was really tense. So tense that the injection was really painful. It was like in my head I was saying, "This is fine, there's nothing to be scared of. It won't hurt." Then BAM! It hurt! And my fear came right back.

Fast-forward a few years, and I've not been training for long in the technique the Head Trash Clearance Method is based on, Reflective Repatterning. I'm at a hospital for one of my early prenatal appointments. Quite early on in the appointment, I'm told that I need to have some injections. Immediately my eyes pop out on sticks and my jaw drops to the floor.

I explained that no one told me that I would be having injections and that I normally need time to prepare. This was a bit of a lie. All I would have done was spent the last twenty-four hours in total and utter panic "preparing." The nurse looked at me and said, "Oh, don't worry; it's not straightaway. We have to get all the needles ready first." Gulp! *"ALL THE NEEDLES READY?!"* And with that, she opened the door, showed me a seat in the corridor, and asked me to wait.

At this point, I could hear my freak-out galloping down the corridor and heading straight for me. But then I remembered. I had just trained in this new therapy, and on the training course, it had been made pretty clear that this technique ate fears for breakfast.

I remember talking to the technique like it was some floating vision of God in front of me. I imagined myself pointing to it and saying, "If you're so damn good at clearing fears, let's see what you can do with this, then!" I didn't have long, so I did a super-short version. I had barely finished when the nurse called me back in. She must have remembered my reaction from before because she asked if I was scared of needles. Before I could consciously formulate my answer, I calmly responded, "No. Not anymore." In my head, I did a double-take: *NO?! Not anymore? Who said that?* This was freaking me out. *Did I just say "no"?*

"Oh, that's good," she replied.

What happened next was weird. Weird in that it was different from how my injection appointments usually went. For a start, I remained upright and my face didn't hit the floor. I was shown my seat next to the table with all the needles on it. Was I bothered? No! I calmly offered my super-relaxed arm. Then I noticed that I was really struggling; struggling with the fact that I was calm and okay.

In fact, the most noticeable thing I was feeling was apprehension. Apprehension because this was a totally new experience and I wasn't sure how it would unfold. There was no fear, though. I just wasn't sure whether this was suddenly going to end and my fear would come right back. I ended up talking through the injections (I'm quite chatty when I'm relaxed), and in no time at all, it was all over. Just like that. It was such a non-event. I didn't faint. I didn't hyperventilate. I didn't even break into a sweat. Nothing. I just sat there, calmly being okay.

But the story doesn't end there. For some medical reason, I had to have injections at every midwife appointment, which was probably monthly. Due to the lack of continuity of care here in the UK, I had a different midwife at each appointment. The funny thing is, every single one said the same thing to me after each of my injection appointments: "I don't think I've ever given an injection to such a calm person before." Seriously? Ha! If only they knew. The injection gods were messing with my head, that's for sure!

Let's fast-forward a few years to my last pregnancy. When I sailed right past my due date and was hurtling towards my induction date, I decided to go for an acupuncture appointment. I never really stopped to think it through until I was lying on the couch and the acupuncturist asked if I had a fear of needles. I'd not really considered it and I had to stop and think about it for a while. I remembered that yes, I used to have a fear of ONE needle going into my body. But where did I stand on LOTS of needles? *How come I was lying here offering my body up as pincushion? What was I doing? Was I scared?* I gave this some thought, almost like I was searching my mind to check.

Eventually, I came to the conclusion that I wasn't scared and that this was totally fine; and it was. That's my story of how I overcame my fear of needles.

If only I could take you back to the day that I did the clearance work. On that day, I spent not more than five minutes doing the clearance work and I only had time to do *two* of the head trash clearance mantras: *I love needles and injections* and *I hate needles and injections*. The clearance work happened instantly. I knew this because I was walking straight into a trigger situation. Unlike my NLP experience, this time, the clearance happened in my mind *and* my body. My subconscious mind was ahead of me that day when it responded more quickly than my conscious mind was able to, which was left confused by what had happened. My body had also experienced the shift immediately; my arm was completely relaxed, which meant that I didn't even notice the needles going in.

Now, I'm not saying you can expect that kind of speed with all things that you work on. A fear of needles is quite specific, and for me, it wasn't tied to anything else, like a fear of blood, for example. Most things we work on will tend to be more complex than that, and they'll need unpicking and untangling so that you can get to the root of it.

What I want to make clear in sharing this story is the speed of the change in terms of how quickly it can occur. What's less speedy is the time it takes to untangle your fears so that you can actually name them, and then the time it takes to clear them. Most things take around ten to twenty minutes to clear, but then you have to work on the opposite, which is another ten to twenty minutes or so. And then you have to keep going back and doing more clearance work.

Just like going to the gym, it's not an overnight thing, especially if you have a number of stresses, fears, and anxieties and you're not quite sure what they are. When I'm working with my clients, they often feel so confident using the technique that they get on with the clearance work themselves; most of them choose to spend their time with me unpicking their head trash and trying to figure out what's hiding in there.

Should I work on the emotion or the trigger?

A great way to think about this is to think of an overflowing sink. The tap is on and there's water going everywhere. It's all a bit overwhelming. The water coming out of the tap represents the emotion that's being triggered by the tap being on (being lied to, seeing a needle, etc.). And as long as the plug is still in, the sink (your system, your body) is holding onto that emotion.

In this situation, to stop the overflowing mess, we can either turn the tap off (work on the emotional trigger) or take the plug out (clear the backlog of trapped emotion). Sometimes, it's just quicker and easier to pull the plug; if anything, it gives you a bit more breathing space to deal with turning the tap off. But turning the tap off first works too.

When to work on the emotion

- When you're feeling overcome with emotion and you just need to calm down and let some of it go. Perhaps you can't think clearly enough to figure out WHY you've been triggered, and your emotion is getting in the way and clouding your judgment.
- When the emotion is stuck in your system and it's always cropping up in some shape or form regularly. For example, *frustration* might need to be cleared if you're always frustrated: frustrated by missing the bus, frustrated by not finding a parking place, easily frustrated by friends or family, frustrated with yourself over lots of little things.
- When the emotion is being displayed disproportionately for the situation, phobias are a good example.

When to work on the trigger

Working on the emotional trigger offers more lasting impact. Also, one trigger point might result in a range of emotions, so it can be quicker to work directly with the cause of the emotional feelings, rather than with all the individual emotions.

- Once an emotional trigger has been identified and it's something that's likely to crop up in the future, then it's worth working on.
- If a situation has taken place in the past that has created excessive emotion, and it continues to do so as you think about it today. Working on the trigger can help you to make peace with what happened and will help to reduce the relentless replaying of the situation in your head. It will also help you to let go of it more easily.

My score hasn't gone down! What am I doing wrong?

If after doing a clearance session, your score hasn't gone down, then there are two possibilities;

1. You need a deeper level of clearance
2. You've revealed a new layer to your head trash

You need a deeper level of clearance

Basically this means that you need to go back and do some more, or, to put it another way, stay longer with the mantras while holding the TAT position. You'll know if this is you because you'll still feel quite intense with the exact same issue. So if you've just been working on being lied to, and you still feel 9/10 on being lied to, then you need to go through the clearance again. Check that your mantras have had the head trash added correctly and go through it again. You shouldn't need to do the clearance more than twice so if you have then it's the next thing....

You've revealed a new layer to your head trash

Let's say you began by working on how you felt as a result of someone treating you in a certain way. Perhaps you were frustrated at how someone was ignoring you. When you connected to that moment of being ignored and tuned in to how you felt, you decided that frustration was it. And out of 10, you were 9/10 frustrated.

Let's say that if after dong the clearance work, you connect back that moment of being ignored. You tune in to it and how you're feeling and you decide that you're still a 9/10. The thing is, you were working on clearing the emotion, but you're connecting to the trigger; you spent your time clearing frustration, but in reviewing what your score, you connected to how you feel from being ignored. When you check your score at the end of doing the clearance, you need to check in with the thing that you were measuring at the beginning, in this case: frustration.

When I'm with my clients, I might now ask them: "How *frustrated* are you feeling?" Typically, the response is something like, *"Oh, now, I just feel really angry!"* So, it's not **frustration** that's a 9/10, but *anger*. In this scenario, we've revealed the next layer, which is anger. There may well be other layers that reveal themselves too; in fact, this is quite normal. It's quite rare for your head trash to be this one isolated thing. Usually, we have these interconnected layers that need peeling back one by one. Our emotions are complex and intertwined. And when clearing one, you're creating space for another one to rise to take its place. Be okay with this and just continue with your clearance work. The more you clear, the easier it gets.

I hope that you now feel prepped and ready to crack on with your clearance work. You only need to try this once to understand whether it's going to work for you. Here's what Jackie, a coun-sellor wrote to tell me when she had read my book;

> *"I've done one fear clearing since reading the book and was amazed at the response I got. I can't wait to be able to do more clearings"*

What are you waiting for?

Resources that Accompany this Book

As I've mentioned throughout this book, I have created some resources to help you on your head trash clearance journey. These include:

- Handy one-pager summary of the clearance method
- Head Trash Clearance Sheet
- BONUS Clearance Mantras

To access the resources area sign up here:
www.clearmyheadtrash.com/book-resources-sign-up

Join the Facebook group

Don't forget to come and join the Facebook group and enjoy the support from a community of people who are already doing it.

You can join here www.clearmyheadtrash.com/Facebook

Can I Support You?

If you would like me to support you on your head trash clearance journey, then book a free chat today.

To book some time for us to speak please visit http://alexialeachman.com/book-chat

Send me an email!

If you would like to email me then feel free to send an email to

hello@headtrash.co.uk

I love receiving listener and reader emails!

Acknowledgments

Huge gratitude to Chris Milbank, the rebellious genius and inspiration who founded Reflective Repatterning, and who encouraged me to take it forth into the world and make it my own. Thank you for your guidance, inspiration, wisdom and healing.

I want to give a huge thank you to all my podcast listeners and to the members of my Facebook group. Your emails, posts and questions have helped me more than you know. I've learned so much from you and I'm so grateful for your support and cheerleading.

Massive thank you to Shaun Hopkins who is never far away for me to think things through.

Big thank you to my dad for being an early reader of the book and help get it into shape.

Lots of high fives go to Coris, Martin and Andy who've offered much needed guidance upon important aspects of the book.

About the Author

Alexia is a therapeutic coach and host of two award-nominated and chart-topping podcasts; *The Head Trash Show* and the *Fear Free Childbirth podcast*.

It was the mess in her own head that propelled her to search for something, anything, that would help her find peace and happiness. Thankfully she found it and not being one for keeping things to herself, she shared what she learned through her podcasts.

She now helps others to clear their head trash with her private sessions, her online programmes and products, and of course her podcast.

Alexia lives in the middle of England with her partner and their two daughters.

www.alexialeachman.com

Also by Alexia Leachman

Fearless Birthing: Clear Your Fears For A Positive Birth

Fearless Birthing: Clear Your Fears for a Positive Birth is your essential road map to confront and conquer the fears that stand between you and motherhood. Through Leachman's unique fear-clearance method, you'll learn how to mentally and emotionally prepare for the birth of your bundle of joy. By ridding your fears, you'll turn potential trauma into an empowering experience.

Fearless Birthing is a must-have guide for expectant mothers. If you like step-by-step instructions, no-nonsense advice from a leading expert, and access to a wealth of online resources, then you'll love this book.

Publisher: Mankai Media

ISBN: 978-1-9998915-0-3 (Ebook)

ISBN: 978-1-9998915-1-0 (Paperback)

Alexia has contributed to the following book;

Childbirth, Midwifery & the Media

This edited collection - one of a kind in its field - addresses the theoretical and practical implications facing representations of midwifery and media. Bringing together international scholars and practitioners, this succinct volume offers a cross-disciplinary discussion regarding the role of media in childbirth, midwifery and pregnancy representation. One chapter critiques the provision and dissemination of health information and promotional materials in a suburban antenatal clinic, while others are devoted to specific forms of media – television, the press, social media – looking at how each contribute to women's perceptions and anxieties with regard to childbirth.

Publisher: Palgrave Macmillan

ISBN-13: 978-3319635125 (Hardback)